Basic to Brilliant

The Definitive Guide to Transforming Your People Practices

A Playbook for the Small to Mid-Size Enterprise

Doris Bentley

FriesenPress
Victoria, Canada

◆ FriesenPress

Suite 300 - 990 Fort St
Victoria, BC, V8V 3K2
Canada

www.friesenpress.com

Book layout and design by Julie Block

Front cover photo: iStock.com/fototrav
Author photo: Anna Beaudry, M.Photog.
Stacking rocks photo: iStock.com/imagedepotpro
Binoculars photo: Vitaly Korovin - stock.adobe.com
Puffins photo: iStock.com/HuntImages
Running photo: iStock.com/laflor
Coffee shop photo: iStock.com/SamuelBrownNG
False dragonhead photo: iStock.com/to_csa
People laughing photo: iStock.com/PeopleImages
Macaroons photo: iStock.com/zlyka2008
Business teamwork icons: alexutemov/123RF
Business development icons: iStock.com/enotmaks

ISBN
978-1-5255-2302-1 (Hardcover)
978-1-5255-2303-8 (Paperback)
978-1-5255-2304-5 (eBook)

1. Business & Economics, Leadership

Distributed to the trade by The Ingram Book Company

Table of Contents

Introduction

There is lots of talk about business innovation today—think Amazon, Uber, and Airbnb. These companies transformed their industries with business models that differentiate them from anything that came before. While much can be learned from their success, innovation is not just the domain of tech start-ups, cluster hubs, or amazing developments in science and engineering.

As an organizational leader, the innovation you see more frequently is likely closer to home. You can probably point to the last few years and recite numerous changes you've made to improve the way you do business by launching new product or service offerings, establishing new partnerships, streamlining processes, or introducing new technologies or upgrades to become more efficient, faster, and effective. These advances, incrementally or by leaps, take your business to a new level. Change and reinvention is everywhere. Or so we think.

For all the innovation around us—across business, non-profit, academic, and public sectors—it seems that real gains in productivity remain allusive. People work harder all the time and are more stressed than ever. How can this be?

Over my twenty years of advising, consulting, and coaching (or was that cajoling?) several hundred business owners and their leaders on their people strategies, I've seen the unique path each has taken from emerging start-up venture through various growth phases, to the market leadership many now enjoy. Today, whether they are positioning for growth, expanding into new markets, transitioning a family-owned operation to the next generation, acquiring other businesses, or preparing their organization for sale, their people challenges are only becoming more complex. Some of the complexities are explained by demographic shifts, digital-first workplaces, and the pace of business. These impacts can't be underestimated. Yet, what's often left behind in the transformation agenda is the talent side of the business: the structures, culture, and processes that support the people who walk through the door every day.

How you structure your organization, attract and hire people, onboard and support individuals to perform at their best, and develop talent for the long term is likely the last "system" in your business to have the benefit of reimagination, or at least recalibration. Your people practices may be ignored or forgotten as a frontier for innovation, yet they can be the real enabler—if not the accelerator—that propels your organization to new levels of performance.

I believe that most leaders want to be more forward thinking in their approach to talent, but they may not understand what to do and their role in making it happen. Further, they may think their organization isn't large enough to embrace contemporary practices. How can their small business of fifty people compete on the larger talent stage with one that employs three times as many? The reality is many do, as you'll see in the pages that follow.

Too often, leaders believe that staying focused on the product, service, and customer experience will get their companies to the future, and their people will come along for the ride. That view works for a while, until role confusion resulting from business growth starts to slow down their once "well-oiled" machine. They may try filling a key role and realize that "perfect-fit" new hire is all but impossible to find. Or a recently promoted manager may decide to change the company's marketing strategy. Then there is shock when a top performing sales person leaves for greener pastures. You know how this goes! It's hard enough to tackle the people issues of today, let alone plan for tomorrow. There must be a better way, and there is.

About the Book

This book explores how transforming your people practices from basic to brilliant can make the difference between stalled momentum and sustainable business growth. As a talent strategist, I've identified eight touchpoints, the key places where the organization connects the employment relationship across leaders, teams, and individuals. Each represents an entry point for talent innovation: the transformation to more contemporary and agile people practices, leading to greater organizational effectiveness and business success. High performing and profitable organizations tend to demonstrate excellence, if not innovation, across all eight, even during times of significant change. Here they are at a glance:

Organizational Design: Role clarity creates alignment of the work with the best decision points and communication flow.

Attract and Hire: Great hiring happens with a strong employer brand showcased by effective recruitment marketing and a first-class candidate experience.

Onboarding: The energy of new hires truly ignites with integration activities that go beyond basic orientation.

Performance Mastery: Frequent and informal feedback delivers a more agile approach to performance measurement in today's fast-paced work environment.

Learning Management: Workplace learning is a conscious pursuit that embraces knowledge sharing as part of the daily work experience.

Talent Development: Talent planning and development is intentional and supports the "care and feeding" of leaders at all levels.

Re-recruit: An energizing, inclusive workplace drives high levels of engagement over the long term.

Total Rewards: Beyond "show me the money," rewards and recognition are customized to support individual values and a life fulfilled.

Each touchpoint represents an opportunity for thoughtful reinvention of your approach to talent and the possibilities that come from reimagining your people practices. How does your organization stack up? Is your approach more on the *basic* end of the spectrum—based on traditional thinking and process—or *brilliant*, on the leading edge in philosophy and practice? The chapters that follow will chart the journey from basic to brilliant. Beyond tips and techniques, each chapter provides:

- An introduction to the touchpoint, key concepts and starting points
- Some facts to provide context and shed more light on the topic
- Several short articles (first published on my company's blog) that explore the touchpoint from various perspectives, including key trends and developments
- Checklists that capture the Basic (traditional) practices that have likely got you to where you are today, and the path to Brilliance (innovative or leading edge) that will accelerate the performance and potential of your people
- A profile of a small or mid-size business that exemplifies the touchpoint

The companies profiled were chosen for their exceptional focus on talent and how they've brought innovation to their people practices in cost effective ways that really make a difference. They represent a cross-section of industries, from entrepreneurial ventures to family-owned enterprises, the corporately structured, business-to-business, and business-to-consumer.

Some have shown insight and innovation from the start-up phase. Others have changed their approaches as business growth demanded new ways of thinking. Above all, they know that taking care of business means taking care of people, and that by placing a primary focus on talent, the results will take care of themselves. If they can do it, you can, too!

While each chapter stands on its own, collectively they represent the path to talent innovation and a brilliant experience and future for your people and business. The book doesn't need to be read cover to cover, though it's not a bad idea! Like a flywheel, you can start the journey on any one of the eight touchpoints, which will positively affect all the others. For example, strengthening your hiring practices can flow through to stronger onboarding; advancing learning management will propel new levels of talent development; and knowing what it takes to re-recruit your talent will inevitably lead to a rethink of your total rewards. Review the contents page and select a chapter or two of greatest interest or opportunity for your organization. You can start anywhere.

While the book is written with leaders of small to mid-size enterprises* and non-profits in mind, many of the strategies are equally relevant for mid-to-large size companies, public sector organizations, and human resources practitioners too!

It's always about the people. Your people. As their leader, you need individuals and teams performing at their best and you need to find those "perfect fit" new hires. You need to harness talent and develop them quickly. Whether your organization employs 15, 50, 250, or more, you can't afford to be basic in your approach to talent. Only brilliant will get you to the future. Let your transformation journey begin!

Industry Canada defines a small business as one that employs 5 to 99 people and a mid-size enterprise as one that employs 100 to 499 people.

Basic to Brilliant

The Definitive Guide to Transforming

Your People Practices

"If everyone had to think outside the box, maybe it was the box
that needed fixing."

- Malcolm Gladwell, *What the Dog Saw*

1 Organizational Design

Organizational design and the org chart—its graphical representation—
can be a foundational touchpoint for bringing innovation to your people
practices. For the small to mid-market enterprise, creating a useful org
chart can be an ongoing challenge. It's the one thing most leaders know
they need to have, yet tend to ignore once it's in place. Why is this so?

When an organization grows, things that were once simple to do
become more difficult. A group of six, ten, or even fifteen or twenty
can manage to keep fluid with quality communication and common
understanding of the business, wear many hats, and do whatever it takes
to get the job done. As the business scales though, communication and
decision-making become problematic without some specialization,
organizational structure, and managerial process. Initially this looks
like adding complexity, but without it, the entrepreneurial venture will
forever remain in a state of chaos.

Where to start? Specialization is usually first. Initially, everyone plays the role of a Swiss army knife, trying to add value in every situation. Scaling the business requires a major shift, where people belong to teams and hand-offs to various groups begin. Instead of sales to project management, you now have sales, estimating, project or production planning, accounting, customer service, and so on. Knowledge now becomes specialized rather than common. New hires can get up to speed fast in this scenario, as there are more people to assist in making sure the learning curve is sequenced and logical.

From here, organizational design takes shape. When done well, it provides focus to communication pathways and decision points. On the surface, it makes sense why a graphical representation of the design matters:

- It clarifies reporting relationships and how workflow is organized
- It helps everyone understand where the decision-making points are
- It helps bring order to chaos in the face of fast organic growth
- It helps make hiring decisions more methodical
- It shows new hires and current staff where career growth opportunities may be
- It can be a lifeline for educating new hires on how the organization is designed, and where each person and role fits into the business structure

Many business owners believe they should wait until they get to a certain size before documenting a structure. However, it's better to do so earlier and add new people to an existing chart than to try to create a chart based on an already complex team and ways of working. Creating this sooner rather than later helps avoid mistakes that can really hamper productivity: organizing work around personalities or agendas, and assigning responsibility without authority. In addition, an earlier attempt can help to avoid organizing the company around products or services when a regional layout may be better.

Whether your org chart needs a dusting off, a do-over, or requires minor tweaking, you can drive more value by keeping two foundational principles in mind. One is that organizational design should represent the communication architecture of your company. Design the organization for the people doing the work, not their managers. Too often organizations are structured to match the ambitions of the people at the top rather than the communication paths needed for people on the front line doing the work. People who need to communicate regularly should report to the same manager. The second principle is that the org chart should be a decision-making matrix for your organization. Consider the types of decisions that are made most frequently and how you can designate the maximum number of decisions under one manager. Effective decision-making and communication need to run on parallel tracks as the further away people are on the org chart, the less they will communicate. The structure of your company will be significantly enhanced by considering these realities of how people connect in the performance of their work.

There are inevitable problems with org charts, hence the resistance to having something so important. The resistance usually comes from the perception of the document as static, rarely updated, and therefore not used as the real-time resource it can be. The other point of resistance comes from the fact that these charts don't do a good job of representing the structures of new generation companies.

Today's high-growth venture or technology firms are typically founded on cross-collaboration cultures where "teams of teams" organize and disband as needed to tackle projects in a time-sensitive manner. These flat or project-based peer-to-peer structures are set up to foster innovation and creativity, but documenting them is another challenge. Thankfully, there are emerging technologies and software like Organimi, SmartDraw, and Creately that are designed specifically to capture these more agile ways of working, providing greater functionality than earlier generations of charting software such as Power Point and Visio.

Whatever design is represented by your org chart—functional, product driven, matrix, or team-based—remember that when it comes to innovation, ideas can and should come from anywhere. The push for creativity and collaboration is forcing traditional structures to reform in favour of more open systems that make companies more adaptable and responsive to change.

Some Facts about Organizational Design

> Many small businesses start with a flat structure where everyone wears many hats and communication is relatively straightforward. With growth, decision-making slows down because everyone has to weigh-in to accommodate this democratic structure. Eventually, decision points with clear lines of authority will be essential for the business to function optimally.

> In matrix organizations (and other structures) where collaboration is key and individuals report to many masters, position profiling is essential to clarify individual accountabilities, decision rights, behavioural expectations, and metrics for success. Position profiles describe roles as they should be, including the collaboration points between them.

> Job design that supports team-based work, information sharing, and opportunities to learn from others enhances employee well-being and output.

> The most effective job design supports individual decision-making and flexibility in how work gets done, which are key indicators of a high-performing workplace.

> Improvements to innovation and productivity can be realized through job redesign that taps deeply into employee talents. This means paying attention to how challenging the work is and how much influence and task-discretion is required.

The New Reality of Contemporary Job Design

Consider the following scenario. Eric was hired as a product manager for a growing technology company and was excited to start his new job. The company was growing into new markets and territories, and offered exciting long-term career growth opportunities. During the hiring process, Eric received a brief description of the position, but within six months, he found his days were filled with some of the tasks he thought he was hired to do, as well as many others, including significant design work. By the end of his first year, he no longer recognized the position he thought he was hired to do. His manager was aware of the changing circumstances surrounding Eric's work; however, when it came time for

Role clarity has emerged as a key factor in helping people understand how their individual efforts contribute to their organization's success.

his annual review, both were at a loss as to how to assess his performance because the position had changed so much. Eric's primary request when they met was for role clarification. His manager wasn't sure exactly where to start to create the clarity Eric needed.

Role clarity has emerged as a key factor in helping people understand how their individual efforts contribute to their organization's success. When new jobs are created, or existing jobs evolve, or the work itself changes dramatically, both employees and managers can be at a loss as to how to validate what they do relative to the changes going on in their work environment. Leaders want to deliver clear job expectations while maintaining flexibility in an environment of continuous change. It's a challenge to make job design relevant in a way that optimizes an individual and company's ability to support current business needs. Streamlined models, tools, and processes are needed to translate the work that people do into contemporary job design.

It's essential to move away from traditional job descriptions that remain commonplace in many workplaces. Those detailed documents once captured every task, from the processes to be followed to the title of reports to be completed. During an era of relatively stable corporate structures and long-term continuity, this was appropriate when a description may have served its purpose for five years or more.

The nature of work today requires a flexible process that captures the essence of the role, while not limiting the document's shelf life with unnecessary detail. The most contemporary approach is to solicit the input of one or more current incumbents, along with those who manage the position or have key interactions with those doing the work. The conversation provides an opportunity to reflect on the organizational capabilities the business is trying to develop and the impact on the work people do. The resulting document should be a profile that describes the purpose of the role, key accountabilities, success measurements, and the competencies required to perform the job at the full working level.

From this base, a recruitment strategy, an onboarding plan, performance milestones, learning and development pathways, and compensation ranges can be developed. Reviewed annually and modified as needed, the document becomes a living, breathing representation of the important work of the business and the measures of success.

Talent Mapping Your Business

Successful business strategies are only complete when they incorporate both a short and long-term vision for your organization's talent needs. Talent mapping can be an invaluable tool for articulating that vision and making it a reality.

Initial attempts to map your talent may have you looking at the existing roles within your organization, evaluating who currently fills them, and contemplating who could fill them in the future. Talent mapping is more than a process of collecting names from your database and slotting them in next to speculative job titles. The process should begin with an analysis of where the roads merge between your map for business growth and your valued employee's career potential based on their aspirations, competencies, and interests. This will take time, communication, and flexibility. If your mapping can be refined to fit both the individual and organization's vision for the future, you've hit the sweet spot.

Talent takes on many shapes, and the key to a robust talent mapping strategy is creativity. Your business needs, current and future, should remain at the forefront of your planning. By balancing strengths on the current team with the gaps that need to be addressed, you might find some promising solutions right on your own doorstep.

For example, if you have someone who is great at both sales and recruiting, creating a hybrid role may be the best route to high performance for that person. What are the risks involved with relegating them to only one function and then going outside to hire for the other one? Is there a better way that you could allocate your resources and support this person as they handle both responsibilities? Great organizational design puts business needs first, but in the small to mid-size enterprise, the reality is that retaining and developing key individuals who add value because of their broad or particularly unique skill set can work to the long-term benefit of the business.

Another situation that can arise when you have a leader who is excellent at all parts of their job *except for one*. Is there a way to move that particular responsibility to someone else? Sometimes we dim the shine of a star by trying to get all five points to be an equal length, but perhaps it's their lopsidedness that makes them a star and creates a winning combination of attributes that would be difficult to find in another individual.

Too often we see an effectively functioning team torn apart because employees have grown beyond their traditional job titles. There are many

> **By anticipating what you'll need, understanding what you have, and exploring where you can be flexible, the talent map can be a dynamic tool as it takes shape to move you and your people forward.**

ways to utilize and develop people's burgeoning areas of competency that will strengthen their level of engagement and commitment while meeting short and long-term business needs. Often, permission to expand beyond an aging job description and the resources and support to be and feel successful can work wonders to keep your people engaged.

Do your homework and have some frank conversations with your best people about where they feel they can add value to your organization in the future. Be clear about your vision and listen closely to how well they are aligned. By anticipating what you'll need, understanding what you have, and exploring where you can be flexible, the talent map can be a dynamic tool as it takes shape to move you and your people forward.

Organizational Design from Basic to Brilliant

Strong organizational design reflects strategic objectives and facilitates alignment of the work with the best decision points and communication flow. To support the design, position profiles document key accountabilities and expectations.

Assess the Basics:

> The org chart, if there is one, is usually created from a hierarchical, functional, divisional, or product organizational design, even if the way real work is done may have changed.

> The org chart is a management tool and is not normally shared with everyone.

> Updates to the org chart are made only when a major reorganization takes place, or when a key person leaves or is hired, rather than undergoing review on a regular basis or as part of a company's strategic planning process.

> Job descriptions are a list of tasks and responsibilities and not reflective of the way the work is actually done.

> People with long tenure at a company may continue to define themselves by an organizational structure designed ten or twenty years ago.

Accelerate with Brilliance:

> Organizational design drives the organizational structure, with the organizational chart as its graphical representation. Consideration is given to company culture and the impacts of technology on the way work is done, ensuring the complexity of relationships are accurately reflected.

> When changes need to be made, managers are briefed and given talking points for communicating to their teams how the revised structure will work and the thought behind it.

> The org chart is explained to new hires to help them understand how the organization is structured, where the decision points are, including desirable communication flows.

> When significant organizational restructuring takes place, people are provided with training and coaching to learn how to operate in the new structure, not left to adapt and find their way.

> Position profiles are updated regularly and describe key accountabilities, people interactions, the measures of success, and the behaviours or competencies required for successful performance of the work.

> Consideration is given to using some of the emerging software applications for org chart creation, such as Organimi, SmartDraw, and Creately, which are ideal for small to mid-size enterprises.

Organizational Design Innovator: CREW Marketing Partners

Established in 2007, CREW Marketing Partners is a full-service marketing agency uniquely positioned as the outsourced marketing department for hundreds of small to mid-size enterprises. From strategic marketing consulting to award winning creative designs, copywriting, web, video, and digital services, they bring a CREW of highly skilled marketing and creative professionals to every client engagement. Under the leadership of founder Braden Douglas and his team, the firm has tripled in size in the last three years, and has grown from a small team at inception to over sixty-five individuals in three locations in British Columbia and Ontario. And that's just the beginning of planned growth to extend their reach in major centres across Canada.

As a professional services firm where talent means everything, designing and structuring their organization through several phases of exponential revenue growth has been an intense learning journey. As a visionary entrepreneur, Braden Douglas enjoyed several years of significant and early success. However, as CREW expanded, he realized he could no longer manage it all. The scope of what was required to grow and manage the business wasn't sustainable by one leader alone. His involvement in the grass roots operations of the business was taking him away from the very expertise he brought as a strategic marketer and chief business developer.

The numbers started to paint the story. Parts of the business were underperforming, and he knew he couldn't realize his strategic goals without the right key people. He made a significant mind shift that many business owners don't make until much later: the conscious decision to create a leadership team comprised of a lead marketing strategist, creative director, and business operations lead. Once hired, this core team became instrumental in creating the foundation for growth. However, each of these individuals had limited people management experience, and quickly hit the wall as the teams reporting to them grew. Chaos was often the order of the day, and the response was to continually re-calibrate roles and responsibilities, while identifying and recruiting new talent.

In the first few years, the marketers and the creatives all worked together as one team, with no real management structure in place. With growth, the size of their one team became cumbersome, so it was divided

> **As short staffing and fluid role definitions became the new normal, staff turnover increased. This led to a realization that if the business was to scale as envisioned, an organizational chart would be the starting point for mapping the roles and talent the agency needed.**

into a "pod" structure, where several marketers and creatives would be assigned a client portfolio, with the writers and designers in a separate pod supporting the entire client portfolio. This was the infancy of figuring out a department structure, and the complexities only increased. While their leaders were phenomenal in delivering creative work through both individual effort and their growing teams, they didn't have the bandwidth to address the operational and business aspects essential to success, such as project profitability and utilization rates. It became clear that these early technical leaders needed a lot more support and structure to be successful.

Nick Bideshi, leader of CREW's Shared Services division (web platforms, digital, video, and copywriting), says that their organizational design was likely typical of small, growing businesses, where staffing consists of moving people around to meet client deliverables today. It was, "Hey, we think this works." It was management by feel. They said, "We need this person to be good at this," rather than looking at the gaps in the business and being more strategic in the pursuit of the right talent to fill it. At the same time, much of the hiring was looking for the unicorn candidate who could do everything. As that candidate didn't exist, they lost a lot of valuable time due to unsuccessful recruiting.

As short staffing and fluid role definitions became the new normal, staff turnover increased. This led to a realization that if the business was to scale as envisioned, an organizational chart would be the starting point for mapping the roles and talent the agency needed. Once the first iteration of the chart was in place, when new team members were hired,

Documentation of position role profiles gained in importance as it became evident that. . ."Without clear expectations, you can be shooting in the dark."

they had clear role expectations. In addition, they were hired on the understanding that the agency was committed to their long-term success in the business, even though at present, there was no identifiable path beyond the first year. Openness on their part to role adaptation would be essential.

As new clients were engaged and teams shifted, revised organizational charts were created to show new communication links and reporting lines. Sometimes a new chart would be issued every few weeks as the structure of the agency changed. While this transparency is a core value of the business, the lessons learned from that time was that little or no consideration was given to how these changes would affect individuals personally. There could be opportunities for promotions, or perhaps job titles would change, but the business was moving too quickly for this emerging leadership team to pause long enough to enroll individuals in the reasons for the changes and what that would mean for them.

Documentation of position role profiles gained in importance as it became evident that, as Bideshi describes, "Without clear expectations, you can be shooting in the dark." They went a long way to providing clarity on the scope of work, the performance expectations, the success measurements, and the people connections—the key internal collaborators who support each position. Today, agency leaders are more confident in showing how the roles all fit together, and monthly off-site management meetings provide the forum for discussion and regrouping. There's clarification of where things stand, what to expect next, and above all, getting to agreement on the next iteration of the org chart.

Naturally, the organizational structure continues to evolve. The agency has acquired two boutique creative firms and continues to enjoy organic growth. A palpable shift occurred when the new role of VP Finance and Administration was added, giving strength to the financial management of the business, along with considered planning for the next growth-phase. The org chart continues to change every few months (instead of weeks), providing new levels of stability and predictability as teams are formed and normed to deliver on their mandates through new levels of collaboration and communication. Team training in soft skills has helped create a common language.

New challenges have surfaced when it comes to promoting individuals and identifying the skills required to be successful at the next level. As happens in many growing companies, strong technical talent would be promoted to supervisory or team lead roles, and these moves don't always work out. It's a work in progress to identify where individuals can be best placed as business expansion continues to serve up more opportunities for professional growth. Bideshi aptly sums up the most important insight of all: "Putting people in the right positions has been the most impactful accelerator for the business."

"It's unreasonable to think you'll find great people if you're spending the minimum amount of time (and money) necessary to find people who are merely good enough. Building an extraordinary organization takes guts. The guts to go to ridiculous lengths to find, keep, and nurture people who care enough to make a difference."

- Seth Godin, marketing guru

2 Attract and Hire

Every business process is changing today, and successful recruiting is no different. The goal of traditional recruitment has always been to get people in the door as quickly and affordably as possible. The rush to fill positions rapidly is often a reactionary approach and administratively focused: get the job posting out, screen resumes, schedule interviews, make decisions. There's a business case for moving beyond this traditional model of recruiting to one that drives business outcomes, truly makes a difference, and brings brilliance to your organization.

Attracting and hiring great people needs to be a much more thoughtful endeavour than it's been in the past. Today's candidates have become increasingly savvy about what they need from a potential employer. As a result, recruiting can no longer focus solely on the shortage of critical skills or the need to fill positions quickly; it requires keen attention to the candidate and new hire experience, supported by investments in more innovative tools and technology. A more considered process is accessible to all, including the smallest business, non-profit, or growing mid-market enterprise. Organizations of all sizes must be prepared to meet candidate expectations and provide better communication, consistency, and transparency throughout the hiring process.

Here are three strategies that drive a more brilliant approach:

Leverage technology. Social media can serve as a powerful recruitment tool, yet many companies have a lot of work to do to optimize its use in this context. Honing your organization's employer brand through the company's website can make a world of difference in becoming a recognizable, reputable, and trusted employer that draws both active and passive candidates. Aligning your online recruitment efforts with your company's marketing function will ensure consistency in messaging and expand your reach to the right candidates.

Focus on the candidate experience. Rethink your approach to candidates and treat them with the same level of attention you give to your customers. In many cases, such an approach requires a different mindset altogether, with new communication plans in place and more innovative tools, too. This focus on the candidate can help solve many of the critical recruiting challenges organizations face today. Are you acknowledging the inquiries and applications of each person who expresses interest in working for your company? For those candidates you interview, are you keeping them apprised of where they are at in your process and what your next steps will entail? Do you know why they want to work for you?

Think—and act—holistically. Hiring well is arguably one of the most crucial people practices in your business strategy. Many companies don't take a holistic approach to their recruiting and hiring efforts. Too often the concept and promotion of the employer brand, sourcing, screening, assessment, hiring, and onboarding are all separate processes with fragmented solutions, handled by separate departments or individuals. How well do your practices work to create a seamless and successful candidate experience, and a positive step forward for your organization? What about the successful candidate's new colleagues and customers? To truly measure your company's efforts to make high quality hires, the full cycle of scouting to onboarding talent must be well coordinated and communicated across the teams and individuals who need to be involved and will ultimately benefit.

The cost per hire and time to fill positions is no longer the gold standard for successful recruiting. It's the quality of process, as described in the three strategies above, that lead to brilliance with perfect-fit new hires, every time.

Some Facts About Attract and Hire

> Winning at hiring can deliver significant returns. If the right managers are selected, an organization can achieve 27% higher revenue per employee than the norm. If the right individual is selected for a specific role, that will add another 6% revenue increase per employee. If you can get selection right, your organization should have 33% higher revenue potential (Gallup).

> There are three candidate sourcing channels that, when used simultaneously, lead to the most recruitment success: employee referrals, online job boards, and social network sites (McQuaig Institute).

> 30% of all Google searches are employment related (300 million per month) (business.com).

> Job seekers spend on average ten to fifteen seconds scanning a job posting before moving on to the next (monster.com).

> 95% of job seekers, whether they are referred to your organization, responding to a posting, or researching new opportunities, will have their first interaction with your company through your website (Bernard Hodes Group).

> 52% of organizations that prioritize the candidate experience saw increases in revenue of 10% or more (Brandon Hall).

> More than 50% of job seekers receive no response to their application at all (Talent Board).

> Efficiency metrics, such as the time it takes to fill a position, are associated with an increase in hiring mistakes by up to 11%. Effectiveness metrics, such as quality of hire, are associated with an 18% decrease in hiring mistakes. Organizations that prioritize quality over quantity realize the most benefits (IBM Workforce Analytics).

What Smart Leaders Do to Land Great Hires

Not all hiring decisions are equal. What makes the difference between leaders who consistently hire rock star contributors and those who repeatedly make hiring decisions that result in a string of expectation mismatches? Our experience points to a philosophy and approach that differentiates leaders who routinely land the best hires.

Here are five things smart leaders do:

1. **They commit to investing the necessary time upfront to getting clear on what they need.** They seek the input of others to create an informed definition of the position and the ideal candidate. This is particularly true when it comes to filling a critical role, such as a management position, key technical expert, or sales professional. They understand that, while they have a vision for what the ideal candidate will bring, there is a need to clarify the position scope, success measurements, reporting relationships, and safeguards to

ensure there is appropriate support for the new person and the new hire. Key internal individuals (stakeholders) are consulted and their perspectives taken into account.

2. **They accept that the right individual may well come from outside their industry,** and not necessarily from "central casting." Transferrable skills and capabilities are most important. Fresh perspectives offered by candidates with diverse experience can breathe new life into their organization, and they know it. In addition, they're willing to compensate competitively and don't attempt to make a lower priced hire to save money while hoping for stratospheric results.

3. **They know when they need a game-changing hire.** This is someone to grow a new line of business or enter new markets, or turn around a failing production plant, or realign an ineffective sales team. Managers have the courage to go out of their comfort zone to bring in the right person to take them to a new place. While there is fear and uncertainty as they are forced to cede some control to such an individual, they know that growth of their business depends on their ability to hire such a star, and then support them so they can truly shine.

4. **They treat candidates as if they are their best customers.** They know good candidates have options as to where they work, and that the interview process is as much an exercise in good PR for their company as it is about selecting the right person. They appreciate that the ultimate decision is two way, and the candidate is choosing them as much as they are choosing the right person. They ensure candidates are informed of what the process and next steps will be, and keep forward momentum happening, even though they may be undecided until the last round of interviews have taken place.

5. **They take a realistic approach when making the final selection decision.** While they may have a textbook wish list of some ideal (and possibly non-existent) candidate, hiring a real person with the experience they need and the right attitude who enthusiastically wants to

work at their company, with all its idiosyncrasies and funky corporate culture, will ultimately be the best hire they could ever make.

We've all seen or experienced numerous minefields in the hiring process. However, when the right person is brought in at the right time, in the right position, in the right company, without fail, the employer has truly done their part to treat the hiring process with the care and attention it deserves. These employers are simultaneously able to build successful and profitable businesses with corporate cultures that are the envy of their competitors.

Five Questions Your Careers Page Should Answer

Did you know that 95% of job seekers will have their first interaction with your company through your website? Whether they're referred by a current employee, learn about an opening through their network, responding to a job posting, or researching companies online, their first and lasting impression of your organization will be made through that initial visit to your site. How well does your company do at managing this front end of the recruitment funnel?

Your careers page (or portal) is the all-important online link for attracting the talent you need. A first step is to make sure your website has such a page or portal (basic approach) to attract and engage potential candidates. It may surprise you that if the page only talks about how great your company is, or only states that you're always looking for great people, it won't go far enough to help them understand why they should make the effort to join your team. An approach called 'recruitment marketing' takes the next step to answer fully the questions that potential candidates have, and in turn elevates the impact of the careers page on your recruitment efforts. Here are five questions your careers page should answer:

1. **How will this company let me know I'm valued?** This is important because one of the main reasons employees leave their current employer is due to a lack of recognition. Your careers page should show quotes or videos that demonstrate the value placed on talent. These could be testimonials or the Friday Fun Days that your company sponsors to show appreciation.

2. **How will this company help me grow and develop professionally?** One big reason employees seek out new opportunities is that they can't grow further in their current position. Top talent in particular seek new challenges, so if professional development is a hallmark of your culture, your careers page should talk about career paths or programs the company offers to support professional growth. If you promote from within, provide examples by posting congratulatory notices of recent internal promotions. If you pay your technology talent to acquire new certifications or pay for management training, say so. This is a big magnet for the best and the brightest.

3. **How will this company's expectations affect my family and my other outside interests?** Workplace flexibility is important today for individuals of all generations, so if this is a corporate value, talk about it. If team members can use flex time to pursue volunteer commitments, or take time for their learning and development, or have flex hours to accommodate personal or family time, provide the evidence. Don't hold back in how that is communicated.

4. **How will this company help me do work that is meaningful and fulfilling?** This, too, is important across generations. So you manufacture heavy equipment or medical devices; how does that affect your customers and the world at large? If there's a social significance to what your organization does, or a clear personal or business difference

derived from the business you're in, let your prospective employees know how the company's purpose creates meaning for those who work there.

5. **How can I be confident this company is worth the risk involved in changing jobs?** Your careers page needs to convey the cultural glue that keeps your teams together. The career risks in making a change are mitigated if an individual knows a potential employer is market competitive on compensation and benefits. Extended health benefits are a given, so talk about the softball teams, Weight Watchers support groups, or gym memberships you sponsor.

The goal of your careers page is to help candidates clearly see that working for your company will help them achieve professional and personal goals in ways that aren't available to them elsewhere. When you

> **Design your careers page from the viewpoint of candidates and you'll notice a significant difference in the quality of those who want to join your team.**

think about filling an open position, it's natural to focus on the skill sets and experience you need in an ideal candidate. However, to get what you need, the messaging needs to focus just as much on what you offer; that is, your employer brand. Design your careers page from the viewpoint of candidates and you'll notice a significant difference in the quality of those who want to join your team. Above all, a strong careers page makes it easier for your current employees to refer the best people, and for the best people to move from passive interest to active candidate.

Should You Promote Internally or Hire from Outside?

Your business is growing and you anticipate reaching those revenue targets you set not that long ago, sooner than expected. As a result, everyone around you is busier than ever and the pace is relentless. You realize it's time to bring on a senior person or people to provide leadership for your growing team. You may wonder if this is the time and how to approach the situation. You have a couple of bright stars on your team—is it time to promote one of them, or should you continue to develop them and bring in the expertise from outside?

One good test for determining whether to go with outside experience versus internal promotion is to figure out whether you value inside knowledge or outside knowledge for the newly created role. Typically, for technical roles like engineering, where comprehensive knowledge of your products and their development may be more difficult to recruit from outside, you may well value the knowledge of your rising stars more than that of someone new to your business.

However, in the case of hiring someone to sell your product to an expanding marketplace, the opposite is true. Knowing your target customers and how to expand your reach globally is likely more valuable than knowing the intimate details of your company's product and culture. This is why, when a technical resource is promoted internally to a technical team lead or manager role, the move is often successful; but when the leading sales person is promoted, it's likely with mixed success. Just because a member of the sales team is delivering outstanding results, doesn't mean they are capable of leading a team, delivering on strategy, or piloting new initiatives beyond where the company is today.

The real reason to hire from outside is to acquire knowledge and experience in a specific area that doesn't exist within your current team. Hiring someone who has already done what you are trying to do can radically speed up your time to success.

When considering an internal promotion, look past current performance and identify employees with the potential to move into future leadership roles. It's likely that those with the potential to go far might not be outstanding technically, but may be those with great communication skills who can handle high-pressure situations or have a real passion to take on more responsibility.

Here are four success factors that can help you evaluate who's promotable and where efforts should be focused to help them strengthen what they already do well:

- **Results** – Usually the first thing managers ask about as an indicator of a great employee. However, key performance indicators (KPIs) and target metrics only measure an employee's success to date and not their ability to meet the company's future objectives.
- **Behaviour** – The 'how' behind performance and results. Any promotional decisions should take into consideration the employee's personality, communication skills, and ability to get results through others.
- **Potential** – Reflects an employee's performance in navigating through situations they haven't been in before, and the likelihood they will suit the business in different roles in future. Potential is a forward measure; it's important to remember that not all high performers have high potential.
- **Motivation/aspiration** – Do individual employees actually desire promotion and leadership development? There is no point forcing an employee into roles they don't want, and if performing well in their current role, they may be best left where they are.

While growth is the goal of many small to mid-size enterprises, it brings with it a challenge when it comes to bringing on or promoting the right talent to drive ongoing success. A highly motivated individual with demonstrated potential who displays unprofessional, inconsiderate, or inappropriate behaviour could be risky to promote. By the same token, the one who always delivers results, is well-liked and respected, but resists new approaches could also be the wrong choice as a future leader. The key is to think big-picture and long-term about your people, and to envision how each of them will behave, grow, and prosper in a variety of situations.

Bringing in the right kind of experience at the right time can mean the difference between strategic success and catastrophic failure. Both decisions, to promote from within and hire externally, can be the difference makers you need at the right time and in the right context.

When Talent Acquisition and Business Transition Meet: Questions Every Investor Should Ask

There's a lot of buy/sell of small and mid-size businesses across Canada these days, as baby boomers advance their exit strategies and move on to other pursuits. As private equity investors do their due diligence, diving deep into product and service offerings and the growth potential of a targeted acquisition, the talent side of the equation is too often a minor or under-explored consideration in the overall buy decision. By asking a few key questions about the selling company's people strategy, investors can gain significant insights into what they might expect once new ownership is in place.

How effective is the current management team in running the business today? How many and who on that team would be key players under new ownership? How aligned will they be with a shift or major change in corporate direction? Those who may have taken the company to where it is today are not necessarily the ones to take it to the future. At the same time, there will be invaluable tribal knowledge that longer-term leaders and key contributors have that could be leveraged under new ownership. Who will stay, who will go, and who will need to be hired requires many truthful conversations to determine the leadership landscape the new owners will face.

What aspects of the corporate culture are essential to the company's current success? This includes the company's brand with both customers and employees. What aspects of the culture need to be changed in order for the company to survive under a new regime? If significant culture change is needed, will the new leaders of the organization have the right stuff to drive new ways of thinking and behaving? Change management is often executed poorly with disappointing results, so any major shifts will require their own strategy and plan, with realistic timelines.

How formalized and relevant are the company's current people practices? What efforts have current leaders made to ensure the way they recruit and retain great people is in keeping with contemporary practice? What is their philosophy around developing people, and what impact will a change in ownership have on key players they'll want to keep? If there is a significant downshifting or sidelining of mission critical people strategies by the new owners, star performers will likely pursue career opportunities elsewhere, ultimately leaving the newly acquired company with a weakened team.

No matter the investor's view of a targeted company's potential, if the people practices aren't fully assessed for both strengths and vulnerabilities, there's a good chance the acquisition won't generate expected returns. Typically, private-equity investors are focused on relatively short-term business results, which can run counter to the behaviours and philosophies of the current organization. Asking these questions during the due diligence process can provide a realistic picture of how their investment interests align with what the seller has on offer, and how well the organization and its people can truly deliver on that promise.

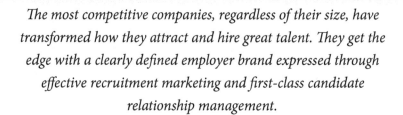

Attract and Hire from Basic to Brilliant

The most competitive companies, regardless of their size, have transformed how they attract and hire great talent. They get the edge with a clearly defined employer brand expressed through effective recruitment marketing and first-class candidate relationship management.

Assess the Basics:

> The hiring process is reactive and event-driven, such as when a resignation is received, complaints about work overload are on the rise, or unwanted turnover leads to a rethink of staffing structures. Hiring is generally a short-term activity to fill an immediate need.

> Job ads are extracted from previous job descriptions, which may not have changed in format or content for several years. The ads typically list job duties and responsibilities, and a standard list of candidate requirements.

> Sourcing applicants is typically through the "post and pray" method. This means job ads are posted online followed by a waiting period where the employer "prays" for the right candidates to come forward.

> While employee referrals may be welcome, there is no formal employee referral program with incentives to reward the efforts of current staff to help recruit on the company's behalf.

> Only those applicants being considered for an interview are contacted in response to their application.

> The process for interviewing and decision-making can vary considerably from one hire to the next.

> Interviews are often conversational in style, rather than a structured approach with targeted questions prepared in advance.

> There is a tendency to interview candidates until one or all of the hiring decision makers select the one they prefer personally, rather than using pre-determined selection criteria that guide the screening, interviewing, and final hiring decision.

> The time it takes to fill a position (efficiency) is the primary measure of hiring success.

Accelerate with Brilliance:

- ▸ The organization's website and social media channels are optimized to attract potential candidates. Clear statements describe corporate values and what makes the company a great employer.

- ▸ The company is open to inquiries from potential candidates even when formal job openings may not be apparent. This proactive practice considers anticipated business growth or succession issues.

- ▸ Leaders engage employees in the recruitment process, encouraging and rewarding every team member in their unofficial role of talent scout. The power of social recruiting—having staff promote job openings through their social networks—is of primary importance.

- ▸ A formalized and widely communicated employee referral program offers financial incentives when they refer candidates who become successful new hires.

- ▸ Job ads have transformed into compelling job postings that creatively tell a story about the employer and the opportunity with the ideal candidate in mind. They are selectively broadcast on social media platforms that provide the greatest visibility.

- ▸ Candidates are treated as if they are the organization's best customers. Applications are acknowledged shortly after they are received and status updates are provided as the interview and selection process unfolds.

> Candidates selected for interviews receive some form of briefing in advance, such as a list of "Top 10 Things You Should Know About Working Here," or a more detailed position description, or communication about the interview process and what they can expect.

> The interview team is well prepared with questions designed to explore the candidate's match with the selection criteria.

> Culture fit is explored through values-based interview questions.

> Both efficiency and effectiveness metrics are used to measure the quality of hires. Efficiency metrics include time to fill, number of candidates, cost of hire; effectiveness metrics include ramp-up time to productivity, performance, and individual-team fit.

Attract and Hire Innovator: Ideon Packaging

Ideas...People...Packaging

In the crowded corrugated box industry, Ideon stands out. They're the premier choice of packaging solutions because of their ability to wow their customers with speed to market of high quality, creatively designed products, and an outstanding service experience. Their state-of-the-art capabilities for design, graphics, and custom-run quantities are housed in their purpose-built 85,000 sq. ft. facility in Richmond, British Columbia. This is where they create, manufacture, and deliver multiple product lines of corrugated containers, stock boxes, protective packaging, folding cartons, and automation services.

Ideon loves boxes, and they love their culture too. It sets them apart from others who manufacture everyday products; they are not necessarily known for being the most exciting places to work. When founder Rick Van Poele launched the company in 2001, he knew from inception that the product and service experience he envisioned would only be realized if the corporate culture was one where staff would love to come to work every day.

He set out to create just that, and today the company's mission, aptly named wow!, defines their desire to deliver more than just an everyday product. Or an everyday employee experience. It's the expectation that their sales, customer service, and design teams will deliver ideas, offer expertise as well as services, and production staff will meet the manufacturing industry's gold standard for quality and safety practices. Today, with over one hundred employees and a staff increase of 25% in 2017 alone, they are one of British Columbia's fastest growing companies.

Attracting and hiring great people to deliver on this mission has been a journey unto itself. Hired as the eleventh employee in 2002, Mike Nunn, Vice President of Operations, has led the evolution of the company's hiring practices. Like many start-ups, early success came from being aware of business opportunities and jumping on them, and then hiring the staff to deliver. It soon became evident their approach to production floor staffing wasn't aligned with business intent. As many manufacturing tasks seemed simple at the time, hiring breathing, warm bodies that

> **The company would start hiring for talent (not skills), knowing they could train people to learn the mechanics of the work. The questions of recruitment strategy shifted to, "What are unteachables the position demands?"**

were physically fit wasn't translating to WOW. New hires weren't the best at communicating or showing the adaptability needed to be successful in their growing facility. Nunn knew they needed a different kind of employee. He turned to several resources to find a better way, learned about a hiring method called "topgrading" and reached out to several HR professionals for advice. Topgrading is an interviewing and selection process that relies on detailed interviews, allowing for more well-educated and evidence-based decision making. This results from a thorough exploration of a candidate's work history, successes, failures, and key relationships throughout their career, creating a fuller picture of the individual's true talents.

This launched a whole new approach. The company would start hiring for talent (not skills), knowing they could train people to learn the mechanics of the work. The questions of recruitment strategy shifted to, "What are unteachables the position demands?" On the production floor, work ethic was at the top of the list, along with teamwork and a willingness to step forward and ask questions. For customer service, detail orientation was essential along with good judgment, a true desire to be helpful and go the extra mile.

With these insights, Nunn and the team proceeded to script interview questions that uncover the attributes required for each position. Next, they established a hiring protocol of structured interviews. These became a blended format of behaviour-based questions that allow the conversation to flow well while gathering a good picture of what makes the candidate tick and their fit with the work, culture, and team.

The final interview has become the most transformational in their approach. It's called a "reverse interview," in which the candidate is invited to spend time in their future workplace. For example, if the person is being hired to work in production, they are invited to spend an hour or two observing production operations, with the expectation they'll ask questions to learn what it's like to work there. Under the guidance of one of the staff, the individual can even try out a procedure or two to get a feel for it. In customer service, the individual can sit beside and shadow the customer service staff as they speak with customers, process orders,

Above all, giving individuals a chance to interview their potential new colleagues is invaluable. "It gets candidates to a place where they can be sure this is where they want to be. It helps them decode if the company is a right fit for them."

and answer inquiries. They can ask questions that will help them understand how the team interacts, anything at all that will give them a full picture of what they can expect. The company is committed to every hiring decision being two-way, ensuring new hires are actively engaged in their decision to join the team.

Throughout the process, there is deep respect for the candidate experience. As Jaclyn Fisher, People Development Lead, says, "We value their time in interviews, so we don't schedule interviews back to back. We get back to people right away on their status and next steps. This is basic in recruiting, but we know many people aren't always treated this way." Above all, giving individuals a chance to interview their potential new colleagues is invaluable. "It gets candidates to a place where they can be sure this is where they want to be. It helps them decode if the company is a right fit for them."

In fact, their interview process has a tendency to embolden potential candidates in their desire to join the team. Most are wowed by the experience. Manufacturing Lead Chris McDonald sees this with most candidates. "We rarely have someone who doesn't walk through the door and not want to stay. They feel the buzz here; it's rare that they wouldn't rave about Ideon."

Where do these great candidates come from? In the early days, their mixed results came from job postings on Craigslist and Workopolis. Depending on the role, employment agencies were used. In the last few

> **Employees have been known to create their own posts with an appropriate image: "I work here doing this, want to join me? Apply now." This makes it easy for employees to share these within their networks.**

years, as Ideon's employer brand has become a real differentiator and celebrated on the company website, there's been a complete shift to employee referrals (with financial incentives) and extensive use of social media. Company events and developments are posted on the company's Facebook, LinkedIn, Instagram pages, and Twitter feed, along with current career opportunities. Employees have been known to create their own posts with an appropriate image: "I work here doing this, want to join me? Apply now." This makes it easy for employees to share these within their networks. At the same time, they are also protective of the culture, and will decline to make a referral if they may know someone but don't think the person is the right fit.

Another prime source of recruiting is internal job moves. There are regular and open conversations between managers and their team members about their development interests and aspirations. This information is considered in the context of overall staff planning, so when positions come available (largely due to growth), there's no secret about who may fit and be interested in making a move. Their staffing process is proactive as a result.

Individuals are given opportunities to explore positions of interest, kind of like an in-house reverse interview. For example, a production worker wanted to become a driver (they have their own logistics team) so the company had the individual see first-hand what their drivers do every day. They paid the individual a couple of hours of overtime to test out the team by spending time with a driver as he drove his route, saw who the driver interacts with on a typical shift, how he manages at the docks and tracks deliveries. This reality check helps the individual make

> "Never settle when you're hiring, no matter how long it takes." At the same time, if a candidate is an awesome fit and that's evident right from the first interview, they don't hesitate to expedite the process.

the decision about taking on the role if formally offered. Similarly, the driver can add perspective on the individual's suitability. It's a win on all sides. Parallel experiences are offered with the design team, sales, and production.

While they generally have prime candidates to interview, they maintain their due diligence with every hire. Not long ago, they went through three rounds of candidate interviews over several months before settling on a finalist. The individual chosen has been an outstanding hire. Everyone knows Mike Nunn's mantra: "Never settle when you're hiring, no matter how long it takes." At the same time, if a candidate is an awesome fit and that's evident right from the first interview, they don't hesitate to expedite the process. The results are wow—brilliant by any measure for any industry. It leads to a highly engaged workforce, minimal turnover, and a business that's profitably expanded entirely through organic growth, one employee at a time.

3 Onboarding

Onboarding can be described as everything an organization does to ensure its newest employees are engaged, supported, and inspired beyond the first exciting few weeks and remain so for the long term. As work complexity has increased over time, a minimal job orientation process for new hires is no longer sufficient. Today's process of onboarding encompasses a more comprehensive introduction to the work and integration with the team, the organization, and the business. However, it's surprising how often we still see the concepts of new employee "onboarding" and "orientation" used interchangeably. While orientation is a key component of onboarding, the strongest organizations focus a great deal of attention on the fuller, more expansive process. The two have quite different, yet related, goals. Here are the key differences.

Orientation: When we orient new employees, the objective is to introduce and familiarize them with how the organization works from their perspective, and cover the basics of how they need to conduct themselves on a daily basis (how to answer the phones, send emails, go for lunch, and so on). We show them around the workplace, make introductions, provide systems training, take care of payroll and benefits administration, talk about safety precautions, and advise them of their daily duties and regular meeting schedules. The mandate and values of the organization are defined for new employees during orientation, and often an overview is provided about the products and services that generate revenue for the business. Sometimes there may even be a brief and relatively clinical introduction to the company's culture.

Onboarding: The intention here is to strengthen the bond in increments until the new hire is fully established and confident in his or her role. This can take anywhere from one to six months after the original hire date (in executive roles, it can take nine months to one year). It takes time, planning, and regular communication touchpoints for an employee to understand fully the expectations around his or her performance. An onboarding program can provide the tools for new employees to be successfully acclimatized, allowing peak productivity to happen more quickly. It includes introductions and time spent in or learning about other departments or work groups, more indepth understanding of workflows and accountabilities, and above all, ways of establishing working relationships across the organization.

Investing in a cohesive and consistent onboarding process that goes far beyond the basics of orientation will have a significant impact on the retention of newly recruited employees.

Some Facts about Onboarding:

> 87% of new employees aren't fully committed to a new job for the first six months (Aberdeen Group Research).

> 32% of new hires have had barely any onboarding or none at all (Bamboo HR onboarding study).

> The longer the onboarding process, the longer a new hire stays. When onboarding is fully planned and intentional, even the most junior level employees in high-turnover positions are more likely to stay at the company up to three years (SHRM: Society for Human Resource Management).

> Organizations with a well-structured onboarding process benefit from 54% greater new hire productivity, and 50% greater new hire retention (Interactive Services).

> Of the top hundred companies ranked by Training Magazine, 80% use a buddy program during onboarding.

Three Keys to Onboarding Success

Why is onboarding so important? The statistics speak for themselves—it's estimated that more than 25% of our workforce have been working at the same employer for less than one year (Statistics Canada). The reasons for this can be varied. Onboarding, or the lack of it, is a key indicator. It lays the foundation for full new-hire productivity and retention beyond the first year. At the very least, failed onboarding means losing the direct costs of recruitment, which can add up to more than thirty percent of the annual new-hire compensation. As talent shortages continue to be a key business trend, your onboarding process needs to include three essential elements. Let's look at the difference it can make to the success of your new hires.

Promoting the Company's Values. From senior leaders to front-line supervisors, their role as onboarding sponsors puts them at the forefront of all onboarding activities. They have both the privilege and opportunity to tell new employees, "This is what it really means to be a part of this organization." New hires need to understand the corporate values and how those behaviours translate to the work they'll do and their peer relationships.

Further, they'll need to know how values live and breathe across the organization. For example, consider an organization that's focused on innovation as a core value. To demonstrate this value, a senior executive might sponsor a brainstorming session as part of the onboarding process, bringing together new hires with more tenured staff, along with outside experts to address a specific innovation challenge. Including representatives of multiple disciplines might stimulate even more fruitful discussion while introducing new employees to their colleagues across the enterprise.

Linking to Learning. Successful companies recognize an important part of onboarding is enabling individuals to find the resources they need to ramp up quickly to full productivity. Recognizing individuals can digest only a certain amount of information at once, a successful onboarding program provides guidance not only on what to do, but where to get information, advice, and counsel on how to be successful in a new role. A multi-faceted, sequenced introduction to the business cycle and how it works, meeting and shadowing key people across departments and functions, and working on meaningful tasks or projects from the first week forward go a long way to ensuring new hires get the resources they need and have the confidence to ask the right people when they need help.

Building Networks for Success. One reason many new hires—staff and managers alike—give for leaving an organization is the lack of connection they feel to their co-workers or managers. Failure to "feel at home" early on through the support of a mentor-buddy and beyond that to team members and managers is a recipe for turnover in the first year. New staff who establish internal social networks quickly and tap into their external networks when needed tend to perform higher than average and have a greater degree of job satisfaction.

Unfortunately, some corporate cultures, at least implicitly, leave new employees to pretty much go it alone—the onboarding mantra might as well be "sink or swim." If the new hire is in a new position, they'll be especially challenged to learn the ropes when there's no company rear-view mirror to guide them. This is not only a loss for the individual but for the company as well, because new workers can bring new life and perspectives to their new peer group. A focus on network development enables new employees to build the support systems that are critical to gain access to information, develop a sense of trust when addressing sensitive issues, build a common context, and speak the corporate language.

New employees can invigorate a corporate culture, enrich all-important social networks, and stimulate innovation and smart risk taking. Ensuring they have the knowledge, relationships, and support to make these contributions should be key objectives of onboarding; this is a key business performance opportunity for leaders at every level in your organization.

Onboarding Executive Hires: Three Keys to Success

Several recent conversations with newly hired executives and the business owners who hired them revealed some challenges with onboarding executive or senior level newcomers. In one case, the new executive hire seemed perfect for the job. His resume was impeccable. He had all the right kinds of experiences and an MBA from a well-respected business school. When hired as the senior financial officer, there was an expectation that his credentials and experience would give him instant credibility and allow him to hit the ground running. Once on board, it was a very different story.

Even though they were consulted in advance of the hiring decision, others on the management team saw this new leadership hire as a direct threat. They felt that this polished outsider suddenly had the inside edge to the CEO/founder's office. That, coupled with what was perceived as his abrupt style, quickly created a rift between the new hire and the rest of the team. Disgruntled members of the management team questioned, aloud and often, the wisdom behind the hiring decision and the capabilities of this particular person. It soon became apparent to everyone that this was not working. On the other side, the CEO was caught completely off guard by the lack of acceptance of his shiny new hire.

When a new executive is brought on board, there are both opportunities and landmines. After a thorough and considered recruiting and selection process, the investment in hiring can wither away completely if the onboarding phase is not given the same care and attention. There appear to be three inflection points that determine either a successful onboarding experience or plant the seeds for missed expectations on both sides.

1. **From the Start: Recruit Realistically.** Soliciting the input of key managers or internal players in creating a fully scoped position description helps to enlist their buy-in for the hiring process and the selection decision. A brief about the company's history and evolution, along with a description of key challenges and opportunities in the role can be instrumental in communicating the essence of the opportunity with potential candidates. While organizations clearly don't want to scare off attractive candidates, a realistic portrayal of the role lays the groundwork for a productive, long-term relationship built on trust and openness.

2. **During the Honeymoon: Collaborative Communication.** Once the hiring decision is made, communication with existing staff about the new executive's hiring is essential and should be done through a variety of channels. Meeting with the staff as a group to make the official announcement is an opportunity to lay out the key initiatives the new executive will be addressing, convey that the newcomer may or will likely do things differently than they've been done in the past (which is why he or she was hired), and build positive momentum for the individual's arrival. In addition, one-on-one discussions with key company 'veterans' who will be most affected by the transition are essential. Supporting the new executive's success and integration into the business and company culture must be a key expectation of the senior executive or management group.

   Beyond the initial communication, one of the key tasks for new executives and senior professionals is to establish effective networks of support across the organization. It's important to look beyond the formal organizational chart and identify informal ways of building support and coalition for change. The new executive should carefully explore other's perspectives and actively seek out common ground where multiple parties agree, leading to subsequent focus of effort and resources. There will be a desire to show results early and go for quick wins. This is desirable, as long as they don't sacrifice key long-term objectives and relationships.

3. **The Early Days: The CEO Relationship**. The success of the integration period after orientation will often depend on a healthy dynamic between the CEO, other senior leaders (or board members), and the new hire. Establishing this relationship can take some fine-tuning. The CEO or the individual's manager will not want to be seen as lacking confidence in the executive, and therefore will likely manage in a hands-off fashion. Likewise, the new executive wants to demonstrate competence and will hardly want to seek out supervision. However, the first few months are the very time when the new hire most needs help and guidance from the CEO, and other senior leaders (or the board, in the case of a CEO hire).

    It's important for both sides to recognize these natural tendencies and schedule more time with each other from the start. The CEO can help the new executive interpret the culture and its implications. He or she can also collect informal data about other people's reactions to the new executive and discuss any need for fine-tuning.

    Executives and senior level hires often describe their orientations to new organizations as "drinking from a fire hose," as they rapidly try to assimilate as much information as possible in a short time frame. The first few months are the time for the executive to listen and grasp the complexities of a new environment. It is vital that the new executive not be swept away by his/her understandable desire to come across as especially knowledgeable right out of the gate.

    Celebrating past success and valuing key tenets of an organization's culture, while at the same time advancing new ideas and vision, is the primary challenge for senior level hires integrating into new companies.

The ability to discriminate between those cultural norms that are vital and immutable and those that are less pivotal and more malleable is critical. This central theme can assist the new executive to successfully communicate a new vision for the organization and ultimately meet the desired goals for change and transformation.

What to Do When Onboarding Goes Off

The anticipation related to bringing a new person onboard can, on occasion, give way to frustration once the reality of job demands set in. As an employer, you did your due diligence and carefully chose someone with the right mix of experience, attitude, and motivation to serve the needs of your company. So what can be done when there are hiccups? What happens when you and others on the management team begin to ask questions like, "Is he or she really the best person for this job?"

It's widely known that there are significant business costs related to finding, training, and keeping people. Turnover hits the bottom line hard, so when some unsettling questions or concerns arise, we recommend not reaching for the panic button too quickly. Face the facts that you, as the employer, have to be committed to creating the right atmosphere that will lead to success for your new hire and, ultimately your business. Don't ignore your hunches, and don't place blame where it may not be warranted. You've entered into a partnership with the new hire, and you need to do your utmost to hold up your end of the deal.

Here are six ways to get your onboarding back on track:

1. **Ensure formal and informal check-ins are happening at regular intervals.** Even the most experienced and confident among us will have questions to ask and assumptions to validate or negate. This isn't about micromanaging when the person is only a few weeks into the role; it's about making sure they have the support, resources, and information that they need to do their best work. Keep in mind that these check-ins are also opportunities for you to let the new hire know what they're doing well.

2. **Don't assume that the person's level of experience means they don't require hands on guidance during the first few weeks.** Even if they did a very similar job elsewhere, your organization is unique and they need specific direction and a veteran's insight while they are getting their feet wet. Don't feel like you're undermining or underestimating them by providing concrete direction and training.

3. **Do they have an introductory project to work on with prescribed outcomes?** While it might seem like the new hire needs space to learn and absorb information, they also need to be kept busy. Provide clear direction around a project that can get them doing concrete work early on. Establish a timeline and state the ways that the project will add value.

4. **Encourage connections.** We all need a little encouragement to get outside of ourselves, especially when we are knee deep in a new job. Ask the new hire if they would mind if you to set up a lunch or coffee meeting with key contacts or people that you think will be a good resource or sounding board for them. Include them in conversations and make all necessary introductions for them to feel welcome and comfortable.

5. **Be as clear as possible when defining expectations.** For those who have been with the company for a while, it can be easy to forget how

things look through fresh eyes. Be explicit when you are talking about expectations and outcomes, but do so without seeming heavy handed or demanding. This can be a difficult balance, so involve the new hire in the conversation so that you can glean whether they truly feel the expectations are reasonable and attainable (rather than just telling you what you want to hear!).

6. **Discuss their comfort level with the pace of work.** If things at your organization move in a way that is faster or slower than what they are used to, the new hire might need time and support to re-calibrate. Talk it through with them without judgment for other ways of doing things. Try to find a common ground for a few weeks to allow them to adjust to the pace of work you expect. Demanding too much too soon, or discouraging things being done too quickly, could scare your newcomer away.

Ultimately, some employees just don't ever quite click, but organizations need to put their absolute best foot forward to provide an environment where new hires can find their footing and make their mark. As one half of the employer/employee partnership, being thoughtful about the stage you set for your new people will help assess shortcomings and course-correct quickly if things should get bumpy.

New Owners Need Onboarding Too

We work extensively with business owners or successors in the process of taking over a newly acquired business. The transition can be a rough go as the key individuals and teams they inherit try to adjust to new leadership. Even a year or two in, resistance to the change can remain as the new owners fail to realize their revenue projections or operational efficiencies. How does this happen when the acquisition or transition held such great potential?

When a business is acquired by new owners, whether through a management buy-out, third party sale, family transition, or strategic buyer(s), the early days of the new leadership structure need to be managed with care. If you're a new owner or a member of incoming leadership, how do you onboard yourselves in a way that will engage the current team and ensure alignment with your vision?

Earning and keeping the respect and trust of existing teams and leaders will be essential if this new arrangement is to deliver on its promise. Chances are that changes will be made; you may decide to make some management changes, restructure roles or functions, hire new people, or show others the exit. Before those decisions are made, you'll need to truly understand how the new business operates (in the case of acquisition), and the key players who'll support your efforts from the get-go. You'll need everyone excited about the future and the value new ownership brings. The path to success in these early days is all about communication—the right messaging delivered meaningfully will be essential. Here are four pathways to lasting success:

Lay the Groundwork. Ideally, before the acquisition completes, you'll have a chance to meet the team and show them why the business will thrive under your ownership or leadership. If this is a merger, bringing teams together from both entities is essential to begin the bonding process. You'll need to understand what aspects of corporate culture must be maintained for everyone to embrace this new marriage. When two cultures come together, extensive dialogue should explore the points of common ground and shared values. You'll need these touchpoints as the new reality sets in.

Show What's In It for Them. The one channel every individual watches during any time of significant change is WIIFM: What's In It For Me? Will

I get more responsibility and recognition? Or be asked to do more with less? Will my years of dedication to the previous owners be swept away in the face of a new corporate direction? Everyone needs to understand what's in this for them personally before they'll get on board and leave their skepticism behind. Failure to connect at this level will leave your integration efforts on the doorstep.

Anticipate Resistance and Pushback. Never underestimate the case that will be made against this change of ownership. Even if the business required a turnaround, or new technologies and markets were needed that only new owners could provide, there will be resistance and fear as people adjust to the new reality. It takes time to try on the possibility of an even better future, or alternatively come to the realization this isn't an agenda one can accept, and move on to greener pastures. You'll need to anticipate various scenarios for what may be a long transition and be prepared to repeat the vision for the future and how you intend to get there.

Identify the Best Messengers. Perhaps you're the new CEO or President, and while you're clear on the vision, perhaps you're not the best public performer. Your new CFO or Director of Sales may be the better communicator who can really connect with the team. They may offer a generational connect or have an experience base people relate to. It's not that the CEO or President should ever abdicate their role as a key leadership messenger, but sometimes others on the management or executive team can make the best change agents. If they are relatable and demonstrate openness to the conversations people need, don't hesitate to have them front and centre as you build momentum for this new chapter.

You can't afford to be ill prepared as you take over your shiny new enterprise or assume the reins of a venture once owned by a family founder. Everyone is watching. With a carefully phased approach to enrolling your new team and a diligent effort to communicate as much and as often as needed, your vision for the future will be given the greatest chance of success.

Onboarding from Basic to Brilliant

New hire integration is redefined to extend beyond the first week. It involves contributions on multiple levels by peers and teams across the organization. Getting and staying connected and learning about the business cycle are of primary importance.

Assess the Basics:

› Once the employment offer is finalized, the new hire knows who to contact during the time between the offer and start date. There is communication from a company representative, ensuring the individual knows what to expect on the first day and week.

› Plans are made for introductions and training during the first week and month.

› The new hire has received a copy of their position description, along with an explanation of what needs to be learned as a priority, and what tasks are key to early success.

› A "buddy" is identified for the new hire, someone to turn to for basic set-up questions.

› Employment policies are communicated clearly and provided in written form.

> The new hire's pending arrival and start date is communicated well in advance across the company, or as deemed appropriate.

> The new hire is welcomed in person or online by the business owner/ CEO or senior level individual other than their manager.

> Steps are taken to help the new hire get and stay connected to key individuals.

> The new hire's manager has regular check-ins (daily/weekly) to ensure the individual is ramping up as expected and creating supportive peer relationships.

Accelerate with Brilliance:

> Pre-boarding is the norm—a lunch or additional meeting or email communication between the offer and start date to keep the excitement and enthusiasm of the offer and new opportunity until the individual's first day.

> Onboarding takes a phased approach that may take anywhere from three weeks to thirty, sixty, or ninety days (or longer, depending on the position). It involves individuals across departments and functions to ensure ongoing and incremental introduction to company culture and business process through meetings, informal social connections, and formal communication sessions.

> There is intranet access or an online portal available that is dedicated to ensure employees get and remain engaged with the company and culture. It includes access to training resources, company information, or updates, and may include profiles of key individuals, the organizational chart, and company policies and procedures.

> New hires are invited (or expected) at ninety days to share with their team of peers and management what their onboarding experience has been like.

> Each new hire has an expectation plan that describes the measures of success at various milestones such as one month, three months, six months, nine months, and one year. For junior or entry level positions, it may be a six-month expectation plan.

> New hires are encouraged to invite their friends or colleagues from outside the company to apply for open positions if they meet the qualifications.

Onboarding Innovator:
Mt. Seymour Ski Resort

Mt. Seymour Ski Resort is a family-owned and operated playground for winter recreation, delivering a relaxed West Coast feel in a thirty-minute drive from Vancouver, British Columbia. Located in the Mt. Seymour Provincial Park, the ski and snowboard area's proximity to the Pacific Ocean, eastern aspect, and the high base elevation provide an average annual snowfall of over a thousand centimetres. The ski area's eighty hectares of terrain, which includes forty hectares lit for night skiing, features gentle slopes where beginners will progress rapidly and excel. Advanced skiers and snowboarders alike thrill to the naturally contoured slopes, gullies, tree runs, and terrain parks.

In a time of buyouts and mergers in the ski resort industry, the Wood family has owned and operated Mt. Seymour since 1984 and pride themselves on staying true to the mountain's roots and creating a welcoming family atmosphere. This philosophy is carried out through the whole organization, and is demonstrated with brilliance in their annual ritual of onboarding approximately four hundred staff and volunteers who are passionately committed to creating an outstanding experience for resort guests. It has become the glue that not only keeps staff and volunteers engaged from the time of hire to the first snowfall and beyond, it's the experience that keeps 40-50% of them returning for one or more seasons.

Attracting enough of the right people requires an intense and strategic effort, when the demographic of their typical employee (16-24 years of age) gets smaller every year, along with the reduction in federal government programs that have helped the tourism industry manage the cost of bringing in foreign workers. Numerous strategies are used to widen the net for new recruits, such as a low-cost shuttle service from Vancouver direct to the resort to eliminate the driving commute and parking requirements. Volunteers are provided with an individual seasonal resort pass in exchange for sixty-five hours of their time; a family pass is provided in recognition of a hundred-hour commitment.

Recruitment activity now begins in June, much earlier than the September start of previous years. Applications are considered as they are received, interviews are arranged with the appropriate hiring managers, and decisions are then made. Hiring momentum picks up in September

---

Ongoing communication with each new hire is essential. This starts with bi-weekly emails and phone calls from their hiring manager and equally frequent e-newsletters to the entire Mt. Seymour community of staff and volunteers.

---

and October through several hiring fairs, and weekly dates and times set up for drop-in interviews. The goal is to expedite the hiring process in every way possible without compromising the quality of hire. Once selection decisions are made, the onboarding journey kicks into high gear.

Most businesses don't have the challenge of making hiring decisions and then waiting for an ill-defined start date several months ahead. At Mt. Seymour, it's more important than ever that new hires feel the excitement building for the much anticipated first snowfall and the beginning of the snow season. Ongoing communication with each new hire is essential. This starts with bi-weekly emails and phone calls from their hiring manager and equally frequent e-newsletters to the entire Mt. Seymour community of staff and volunteers.

In mid-November, a full staff orientation and training program is launched, which includes department head training. Each department (ski school, rentals, guest services, food and beverage, and so on) conducts three to six full days of training spread out over several weekends, given that many of the staff and volunteers are students or working full-time elsewhere. The Guest Services and Rentals department training takes place on evenings and weekends over a six-week period.

There are forty volunteers hired for the Resort Host program, and eighty for the ski school. The hosts receive a full day of training, and then each person is paired with a returning volunteer and other staff to work with them until they are fully comfortable with what they need to know. There's a lot of information to absorb to understand the operations of the parking lot and shuttle drop-off, check-in procedures, equipment rentals, tickets; there will be many Q&A's once the season gets underway. Ski-school volunteers are under the direction of an instructor, and full training is provided (at the resort's expense) to meet the requirements

> **Onboarding also requires the integration and alignment of new staff with returning staff, and the lessons of experience here are the more time they all spend together, the sooner the newbies get up to speed.**

of levels one through four of ski instruction. A two-day class includes a mock-up of the tots area, a description of the lesson flow, and what instructors will be required to do.

Traffic and Grounds staff receive two to three days of training (again spread out to accommodate their other work lives). They will face a barrage of issues once the resort opens, as the traffic arrives all at once. There's no ramp-up to appreciate fully what's needed to manage parking flow; once the resort is operating, it's go-time for all.

Onboarding also requires the integration and alignment of new staff with returning staff, and the lessons of experience here are the more time they all spend together, the sooner the newbies get up to speed. Buddy systems operate everywhere, from lift patrols to guest services and rentals. In the call centre, where two to three days of training takes place, new staff work side-by-side with experienced staff to learn the language of the products and services, and become fluent in resort policies.

Training and onboarding tools have evolved over the years and are fully developed for 24/7 online access on their Moodle platform (open source learning software). Training materials are made available for staff review in advance of formal training. While experiential group training is the centrepiece, learning and onboarding is extended through the Moodle portal, where all training materials are posted, their usage tracked, and quizzes administered.

After all the training is complete, a Mountain Orientation Day is held at the end of November. It's an activity-based learning event where all

The intent is that everyone understands the whole operation, so all become ambassadors for an outstanding guest experience. This additional level of engagement creates momentum for a great season ahead.

staff and volunteers move through various stations on the mountain—ski school, toboggan runs, food and beverage, parking, rentals—and under the instruction of a returning supervisor, engage in a ten- to fifteen-minute activity that helps them experience first-hand each area of the resort operation. There are ten groups of about ten to fifteen in each, a great opportunity to meet and greet their peers across the mountain. The intent is that everyone understands the whole operation, so all become ambassadors for an outstanding guest experience. This additional level of engagement creates momentum for a great season ahead.

After an exceptional onboarding investment, what happens next if the snow doesn't fall? There will be yet another social event—everyone will show up for great food—and the bonding continues. Sponsors are present, and everyone receives a sports-related gift such as goggles, glasses, snowboard gear, all the accoutrements needed to feed the anticipation.

The experience is the reward for staff and volunteers alike. To keep the engagement, all receive a complementary season's pass for the remainder of the season after the post-Christmas rush. In February, a survey is conducted to get feedback from staff and volunteers on their experience. It's still peak season then, but the survey is designed to capture as much feedback as possible before staff depart and the season winds down.

The challenges of operating a seasonal ski resort are endless. For the Mt. Seymour Ski Resort, their success is in no small part due to the Wood family and their personal commitment to being there on the front lines during the peak season. It's all hands on deck for the family, in partnership with their dedicated team. They can be justly proud of delivering an outstanding onboarding experience for their extended family of passionate skiers, snowboarders, and outdoor enthusiasts, who thrive on their annual mountain experience.

"Our talent mission is to scale
a human and high performing organization,
one that takes care of people
while taking care of results."

- Rian Gauvreau, Co-founder and Chief People Officer, Clio

4 Performance Mastery

Setting your people up for high performance—or performance mastery, as we call it—is the engine that delivers on business results. However, it can be a challenging innovation touchpoint for many organizations to implement successfully.

One of the keys to long-term leadership and organizational success is moving employees to actions that deliver the results you are seeking. The challenge is that high performance depends on your ability to achieve business goals again and again, often with the same people. How do you get more results in less time? Beyond aligning the work with individual strengths, being clear on expectations, and setting achievable but stretch goals (givens in any high performing workplace), how else can you set your people up for high performance? Here are some of the levers you can use to ensure performance mastery is alive and well in your organization.

Revamp or reinvent your performance review process. If you haven't moved away from the annual ritual of those brutal ratings scales and talking about the past, which doesn't set people up for a brighter future, you're being left behind in a world that's moving fast. Employees are expecting more frequent, less formal feedback. It's time to understand how a shift to performance planning and more agile goal setting can be the key to unlocking the motivated high performance you need from your team members.

Take the time to articulate the measures of success for every position. How else will you or the people doing the work know they are meeting the mark? Even when the work is largely relationship-based and many qualitative factors spell success, knowing what those are is key to helping people stay focused on the right things and demonstrate the behaviours needed to achieve results. Every position needs key performance indicators that should align with the goals of the business unit, and the organization's strategic plan.

Don't be afraid to course correct frequently and in real-time. Your employees will thank you and your business will be better off for it. Don't wait until your next one-on-one or performance meeting to have the conversation you need to ensure your team member is on track and meeting expectations. Whether coaching, mentoring, or motivating, whichever conversation or approach is appropriate, seize the moment when the time is right.

Check your assumptions about what motivates your people. If you don't know your team members well enough individually, you may be making assumptions about what drives them to perform the way they do. For some, it's about being part of a successful team; for others, the sheer love of the task at hand gets them up in the morning. Some will be there for the money, and for many, it will be the challenge and career growth the work provides. Or, surprise, it may be working for you that's motivating them to achieve! Motivators are personal and unique to each individual, and in the pace of business, it's easy to forget what underlies the performance of your best players.

Put compensation and incentives in perspective. When variable pay incentives are in place, some managers assume these will be a key driver of employee performance and will encourage their staff to strive for every dollar they can. Incentives are appropriate for many positions to acknowledge exceptional performance and to share the collective success of the organization with those who made that happen. However, believing in or promoting the use of incentives as a primary motivator of performance often leads to unintended consequences like neglecting responsibilities that aren't incentivized, poor collaboration, and even gaming the incentive system.

Performance mastery can be multi-faceted and it's important to know what, if any, barriers may be standing in the way of your team aligning their best efforts with the business, and how best to clear the path for exceptional performance. When team members know what's expected, have the skills to perform, know what success looks like, and have their key motivators met, the results can be a force multiplier for your business.

Some Facts about Performance Mastery:

> A high performer can deliver four times more productivity than the average performer (HBR research).

> Up to 30% of the variability between lagging performers and top performers can be attributed to organizational climate (Hay Group).

> An estimated 50% of performance problems occur because of lack of feedback.

> Only two in ten employees strongly agree that their performance is managed in a way that motivates them to do outstanding work. Only 14% of employees strongly agree that the performance reviews they receive inspire them to improve (Gallup).

> To live the status of high performer means being open to learning, embracing the new and foregoing the old, being humble enough to replace old beliefs of what was once "right" with new definitions of what "right" means (Jeff Boss, *How to Find Certainty in Uncertain Situations*).

> Without frequent, two-way communication between a manager and an employee, changes to the current performance management practices will be nearly impossible to achieve (Gallup).

> Managers should separate discussions about pay and performance. This allows dedicated time for compensation issues and frees up the performance dialogue to focus on achievements and goal setting without the "fight for pay" looming over or undermining the conversation.

> Feedback and developmental coaching that focuses on strengths and accomplishments motivates improved performance more effectively than traditional approaches focused on fixing weaknesses (Clifton Strengths research).

> Effective performance coaching is based on an individualized understanding of each employee and is delivered through three components: establish expectations, continually coach, and create accountability.

> Companies can raise the productivity of workers by 20–25% by adopting social collaboration tools. A "social" business is defined as one that uses social technology to foster collaboration among customers, employees, and partners (IBM Workforce Analytics).

Why You Should Stop Doing Performance Reviews

The traditional annual employee performance review is the most maligned of business practices. The structures and processes that most organizations use to evaluate employee performance are the same ones that were used fifty years ago. Forms, ratings, and categories may formalize the process (read: make it more impersonal) and produce tidy reports, but they do not benefit the employee's development or improve their performance. Isn't that the reason you're doing reviews in the first place?

Anytime you put people into categories (such as below expectations, meets expectations, exceed expectations), you do them a disservice by suggesting they bring the same level of competence and attitude to their work regardless of the situation. Ranking an employee's ability to "complete projects in a timely manner" as "average," for example, does not tell them anything about how they can develop their time management skills, utilize resources more effectively, or, most importantly, what it is that you expect from them going forward.

The reality is, unless you are managing a group of assembly line staff, performance is difficult to measure on a quantified scale because of the subjectivity of the evaluator and the natural fluctuations and re-calibrations of the evaluated employee's output. Here are some solutions to consider:

- Provide space and time for less formal, more frequent conversations.
- Train supervisors as coaches, not dictators or watchdogs.
- Ask employees to tell you their strengths. Design the workplace around those.
- Address issues in real time and show concern for those struggling.
- Encourage employees to take ownership of their performance standards and results.
- Align employee efforts with overall business goals. Do this often.

The transition from a long annual one-and-done meeting to several short meetings through the year will have a lot more impact and be easier to manage. The reduction of unnecessary stressors and the emergence of trust with your people can only serve to inspire higher levels of performance and in turn benefit your bottom line.

Four Ways Performance Coaching Can Accelerate Your Business

The concept of moving from an annual performance review as a primary means of delivering feedback has given way to performance coaching—a more agile, real-time approach to helping individuals achieve their potential, course correct when needed, and receive timely accolades for meeting or exceeding expectations.

Today, performance coaching is a core management skill. When fully developed, performance coaching allows managers to get and give feedback and feedforward, recalibrate performance expectations, mediate issues between an individual and other(s), collect data and help evaluate a problematic situation, and be a "venting" resource, all within the context of moving to an end result with a positive business impact.

Here's how performance coaching can accelerate your business:

- **Clearheaded Thinking.** Taking time for one-on-one performance check-ins can provide the space for an individual contributor or emerging leader to think through issues and challenges in an organized way. When the check-ins are more frequent, a level of trust should develop between the individual and manager. This allows for more in-depth exploration and understanding of an individual's performance in real-time. Sitting down with a manager who takes a coaching approach can help the individual be more mindful of their impact, with fewer knee-jerk reactions and better management of the unexpected.

- **Communication and Relationships.** The most significant immediate improvements generally happen in the area of working relationships. Individuals who receive coaching support tend to integrate positive workplace behaviours more consciously, and in the case of team leaders or managers, are in turn more likely to use effective coaching skills with their direct reports and coworkers.

- **Performance Gaps.** Even the most accomplished top performers have areas where there is room for improvement. Problems can arise when individuals are unable to define the problems for themselves or feel overwhelmed by what they might view as an insurmountable gap. A manager/coach will invite the individual into a discussion about areas for improvement, ideally discuss together options for moving forward, and create mutually determined goals and a plan for follow-up. Because the manager has partnered with the individual on determining next steps, if and when things become challenging for the individual, the manager is better able to help with motivation, support, and where needed, a push toward reframing the next performance goal and desired behaviours.

- **Confidence.** An individual's personal and organizational effectiveness is ultimately determined by their leadership ability (starting with leading self before leading others). Coaching can encourage the kind of confidence and deliberative thinking that will help individuals work through their challenges, reach beyond their comfort zone, and when times call for it, make tough decisions or embrace difficult conversations. Performance coaching helps them gain a more realistic view of how others see them and how they see themselves.

For some leadership teams and well-entrenched industry cultures, performance coaching as a management approach may sound aspirational or even delusional. Not all managers have a natural coaching mindset; for some it's much easier to wear a problem-solving hat and direct (tell) the individual how to improve or resolve an issue, rather than attempting to work with them to come to an agreed upon plan of action. It takes time to learn how to explore the root cause of what may be holding an individual

> **Performance coaching cannot happen in a vacuum. Integration and alignment with other leaders and the team, the business strategy and an overall vision for the organization is essential.**

back, or preventing them from reaching new levels of contribution, or to providing positive feedback in a way that motivates a team member to improve continuously. However, with training and skill development, most managers can master the techniques of effective performance coaching, increasing their effectiveness and connection with their team.

Performance coaching cannot happen in a vacuum. Integration and alignment with other leaders and the team, the business strategy and an overall vision for the organization is essential. With proper planning and key parameters addressed, the performance coaching approach can accelerate individual and team performance, drive forward momentum, help people grow and develop, and create pathways to new possibilities.

Truth and Consequences: How Managers Create Their Own Poor Performers

A recurring theme experienced by many of the companies I have worked with has been the struggle to address the problem of a poorly performing employee. When an employee fails—or even just performs poorly— managers are often left mystified. Several explanations are offered— the employee doesn't understand the work, or isn't driven to succeed, can't set priorities, or won't take direction. The problem is most often assumed to be the employee's fault—and the employee's responsibility.

But is it? Sometimes, of course, the answer is yes. Some employees are not up to their assigned tasks and never will be for lack of knowledge, skill, or simple desire. But sometimes, and I would venture to say frequently, an employee's poor performance can be attributed largely to the actions of his or her employer.

Unfortunately, the road to poor performance frequently starts when a new employee is hired. A weak or nonexistent orientation to the company and culture leaves an employee to find the way through unproductive activity, often learning much about the company and its people that is not intended. What will the new employee be expected to do by the end of the first three months, six months, at one year? An early discussion of such performance expectations is essential for both the employee and manager to be clear about what the employee will have to learn and do in order to be successful, and to understand where the bar of performance has been set.

When bringing on a new hire, managers must actively direct the individual, gradually reducing their involvement over time. Early guidance is not threatening to new employees (at any level), as it's not triggered by performance shortcomings. It is systematic and meant to help set the conditions for future success. Frequent contact in the beginning of the relationship gives ample opportunity to communicate with the newly hired employee about priorities, performance measures, time allocation, and even expectations of the type and frequency of communication. That kind of clarity goes a long way toward preventing the dynamic of poor performance, which is so often fueled by unstated or unclear expectations.

After the critical first year with a new hire, managers can avoid a journey down the path to poor performance by challenging their own assumptions and attitudes about employees on an ongoing basis. They need to work hard at resisting the temptation to categorize them in simplistic ways. They must also monitor their own reasoning. For example, when feeling frustrated about an individual's performance, they can ask

> Too often, employees and managers alike, typically hear nothing at all. The "no news is good news" approach to feedback and performance assessment can be a recipe for disaster.

themselves, "What are the facts?" They can examine whether they are expecting things from the employee that have not been articulated, and try to be objective about how often and to what extent the employee has really failed. Managers need to delve into their own assumptions and behaviour before they initiate any serious action to remedy the situation.

Employees often think they are doing splendidly. Some managers assume that the annual or semiannual performance review is all the feedback that employees need. Used alone, the formal review process allows too much time to go by before the employee is told what he or she is doing wrong. Realistically, you can't be expected to provide feedback every day on every assignment. But when something important is involved, offering tips for improvement on a point that will have ramifications for future assignments is invaluable when offered sooner, rather than later. Known as feedforward, this helps an individual adjust their efforts to improve results and will be openly received, especially if the tasks are difficult to master or continuously changing. Too often, employees and managers alike, typically hear nothing at all. The "no news is good news" approach to feedback and performance assessment can be a recipe for disaster.

One cannot overstate the case for creating an environment in which employees feel comfortable discussing their performance issues and concerns. Such an environment is a function of several factors: the manager's openness, comfort level with having his/her own opinions challenged, even his/her sense of humour. The net result is the manager and employee

---

You deserve to be using your resources developing employees who can succeed. Your failed employees deserve the chance to get on with their careers in what can be for them, another, more promising setting.

---

feel free to communicate frequently and ask one another questions about their respective behaviours before problems mushroom or begin to surface.

There will be times when an employee is ill-matched to your organization. It could be that he or she is not really suited to your kind of business or your size of firm. It could be that he or she screwed up early and never will get another honest chance to succeed. It could be that you made a mistake in the hiring process. Whatever the reason, the employee's interests, as well as your own, are best served when you bite the bullet sooner rather than later. You deserve to be using your resources developing employees who can succeed. Your failed employees deserve the chance to get on with their careers in what can be for them, another, more promising setting.

Keep Your Young Eager Beavers Moving Upstream

Many organizations enjoy the promise of welcoming freshly minted college and university graduates into their fold. As bright enthusiastic new hires, these bright-eyed keeners can breathe new life into the work and corporate culture. At the same time, if not integrated into the business with care, these eager beavers can inadvertently dam productivity, decelerating performance of themselves and their team members.

How? New next-generation or millennial employees can get antsy. Our culture delivers instant gratification in so many ways, including instant messages, on demand entertainment, personalized learning experiences, customized jeans. New recruits wonder, "Why can't I get instant results at work? I have a great idea that could save this place thousands/millions of dollars, and I've only been here a few weeks. Why doesn't everyone else see it?"

Young eager beavers bring fresh energy and ideas that at first glance may have the potential to generate significant advances in increased productivity, new opportunities, and cost savings. Balancing their great ideas with due diligence and appropriate guidance can be a challenge for any growing organization or one that is undergoing significant change. Eager beavers often don't realize that building a dam at one location might improve the resources and depth of one line of business, but can dry out systems and revenue sources downstream. Each idea should be evaluated for effectiveness in the organization as a whole. More importantly, those ideas—and the talent—must fit with your business strategy and organizational culture. So how do you keep newly hired eager beavers from damming the performance flow without stifling their creativity?

Start with a trial period. All new people, including those who have been promoted or moved into new roles, should be given a trial period in which to demonstrate consistent performance. Trial periods give new team members time to learn and understand culture, key players, and how various business functions interact and collaborate. Set a time frame that allows the eager beaver to learn the needs of his position and allow the manager to see if he can meet expectations and fit with the culture. The last thing you want is a team member who doesn't play well in the swimming hole with others and constantly misjudges the depth of the stream.

Set clear, realistic expectations. When onboarding any new team member, establish minimum expectations for her to meet. If these expectations differ in any way from the job description used to recruit her, point out those differences. If expectations change over time, point out how they will change and the difference they will make. Managers should also be asking if the minimum expectations are realistic for one person to take on. If you set the bar too high, you guarantee that your talent will fail. There's a balance to be achieved between creating upstream momentum and fostering the confidence to continually take on more challenges as knowledge of the work and business increase.

Measure performance frequently and informally. Can the eager beaver meet expectations and meet them consistently? Effective performance by anyone in your organization (new or advanced, eager or experienced) is measured by how well they consistently meet expectations each day. Check in at least every two weeks to compare notes on performance. Are expectations being met 100% of the time? If not, should her responsibilities be revised? More training provided? Or does she lack the capacity to meet the baseline expectations needed for the role? Beavers who can't swim shouldn't be treading water in the hopes they are progressing upstream.

Show them how to link great ideas to your business strategy. Eager beavers should be able to demonstrate an understanding of culture, people, and direction so they can generate ideas that are meaningful to your organization. Without this understanding, ideas are created in a void, without understanding of leadership concerns and market demands. Eager beavers and their supervisors can waste a lot of time living in the land of possibilities, diverting into shallow streams while the rapid-like force of real opportunities require their immediate attention.

Eager beavers and the dazzle of instant gratification can dam performance flow for the core products and services they have been hired to support. If they can show consistently, over time that they can perform to expectations and show measurable performance each day, trust these energetic sources of talent to be creative and innovative in thoughtful, meaningful ways, and deliver on the expectations you had for them at the time of hire.

Performance Mastery from Basic to Brilliant

Traditional performance reviews have shifted from evaluation of past performance to more agile goal setting, frequent and informal feedback, and real-time coaching. Performance assessment and goal achievement happens through regular check-ins, not an annual event.

Assess the Basics:

> If performance reviews are conducted, they are most frequently on a semi-annual or annual basis. They are often connected to a compensation review at the same time or shortly thereafter.

> The feedback process tends to be driven by the manager, with little or no input from the employee. The manager takes an "all-knowing" approach to the assessment of the individual's performance.

> Rating scales may be used to assess the individual. They are often subjective in nature and subject to the opinions of the manager, who may or may not have first-hand experience in observing the individual's performance.

> Performance goals are often directly related to the job itself, and not necessarily aligned with overall business goals or strategic plans. The overall business strategy may not be transparently communicated,

so individuals may not have a full or limited appreciation for how their performance contributes to overall business success.

> Individuals may understand what's expected of them on a daily basis, but may not have a clear line of sight on what defines outstanding performance, or how it will be recognized.

> The reward for high performance is often an increased workload (more of the same), not necessarily new developmental challenges.

> Sub-optimal or poor performance may be tolerated due to either manager inattention, lack of accountability, or skill deficits that impede appropriate action. There may be significant time delays between incidences of poor performance and manager feedback.

Accelerate with Brilliance:

> Team members are clear about what's expected of them and are informed when those expectations change. Key performance indicators (KPIs) are understood and performance attainment is regularly reviewed, tracked, and documented.

> Performance planning is a collaborative process between employee and manager (rather than a manager to employee directive). The formal annual review is nixed in favour of more frequent and less formal performance check-ins, often on a monthly or semi-monthly basis.

‣ The manager style has evolved to one of performance coach, where employees and managers alike actively engage in regular conversations about strengths and how to further develop them.

‣ As performance coaches, managers are effective in providing meaningful and timely performance feedback (an assessment of what's been done) and feedforward (what can be done next to enhance performance).

‣ Poor or lagging performers are given the opportunity and support to improve. If reasonable efforts have been made without success, they are quickly redeployed with other responsibilities or transitioned out of the organization. Poor performance by one individual is not allowed to fester and negatively affect the work environment.

‣ Performance-focused managers set the bar high, build trust, and have faith in their team members.

‣ Team members understand how their performance contributes to the organization's success.

Performance Mastery Innovator: Clio

Launched in 2008 and based in Vancouver, BC, Clio is one of the Canada's fastest growing companies, specializing in cloud-based practice management technologies that improve the quality of practice for lawyers around the world. Clio is an integrated case management software that eases the process of time tracking, billing, administration, and collaboration for law firms of all sizes. Clio's growth from its two visionary co-founders to approximately 250 employees today across offices in Vancouver, Calgary, Toronto, and Dublin has earned it numerous awards such as the Deloitte Fast 50™ and Fast 500™ (the highest-growth technology companies in North America), and one of Canada's Ten Most Admired Corporate Cultures of 2016 by Waterstone Human Capital.

Clio's approach to performance mastery has developed organically from its roots as a budding software venture with a small remote workforce. From the outset, co-founders Rian Gauvreau and Jack Newton invested in chat tools such as Slack and video conferencing that gave them a way to effectively channel activities, exchange, and share information. As new team members were hired, the goal was to create as close to a local employee experience as possible. As the revenue stream grew and investor capital was raised, their growing Burnaby-based corporate office has allowed them to scale to an extremely agile and responsive organization, driving the most robust development and reach of its product offering.

Their belief is that managers are responsible for enabling performance at every stage of the employee lifecycle, from first impression to farewell. They know that while many tech companies boast exponential profit growth quarter after quarter, they can also be known as terrible places to work. Others have prioritized harmony and happiness at the expense of productivity and progress. Clio's co-founders and leadership team are fully aligned in their belief that it's possible to be both human and high performing without comprising the achievement of world-class results. Therein lies their approach to performance mastery.

Based on the realization that most people have a "broken notion of what performance is, such as an annual mysterious event," Clio's leaders and Talent Team work hard to instill regular semi-monthly touchpoints between managers and their individual team members. Managers/leaders have been trained to be highly communicative in how they define

They've changed the language of performance mastery from "evaluation" to "assessment" (what's on your page now) and "acceleration" (where you need to stretch for more success).

expectations. There are three components: what you need to be working on, what you need to work at getting better at, and who should support you. These semi-monthly conversations with every team member provide close to real-time feedback and feedforward on tasks, responsibilities, and individual performance.

The goal in the conversations is to come to a shared understanding of performance, and truly live out that philosophy. They've changed the language of performance mastery from "evaluation" to "assessment" (what's on your page now) and "acceleration" (where you need to stretch for more success).

This level of communication frequency builds openness between the manager and team member that allows both to step up to difficult conversations if required. Their mantra is "radical candor" that doesn't damage the relationship between the two. Because of the regularity of check-ins and performance calibration, there is usually a close alignment between a person's self-assessment and that of their manager. Individuals are never surprised in conversation, and always have a clear sense of where they stand.

As Rian Gauvreau, Chief People Officer and Co-founder says, "Our ability to continuously innovate, fail forward, and learn from one another will determine our success in this grand experiment, but only if we're open to giving it an honest go."

In this environment of innovation and growth, where rear-view mirrors don't exist, the work itself is developmental, propelling individuals

> "Managers are continuously trained and coached to approach their conversations from a place of curiosity about the individual, and a place of deep care and concern." The end state is to see people positively pushed to their limits, and not be broken from it.

to expand their performance and learning far beyond what they ever thought possible. Often individuals are doing things for the first time every day (or every minute), constantly "playing" in new territories. As a company, it can feel materially different from one day to the next. As a result, their performance frameworks have to embrace that reality. Lyndsey Hannigan, Director of Talent, affirms their ongoing investment in supporting managers to be effective performance champions: "Managers are continuously trained and coached to approach their conversations from a place of curiosity about the individual, and a place of deep care and concern." The end state is to see people positively pushed to their limits, and not be broken from it.

What are the tools that enable and track these conversations? Clio uses a tool called Lattice for goal setting and performance management, a place where managers and employees can track inputs/outputs of their one-to-one conversations, and log action items. This provides a living narrative of their performance and development journey.

New employees are given a tool kit so they can learn every chance they get to affirm their alignment with where their team, function, and the company is going, maintaining vigilance about what's changed and what's shifting. From their first few days through the entire onboarding process, newbies are "normed for feedback" and learn the meaning of the radical, candid, workplace conversations to come. They learn how their

> **They wanted to create a disruptive HR organization that would staunchly avoid a heavy lift of process, and continually deploy tools that are lightweight and really serve the organization, not the back-office function that supports it.**

one-to-one conversations with their managers will be structured and the role they play in inquiry and dialogue. Performance conversations are never one-way.

The importance of Clio's Talent Team in the context of performance mastery cannot be understated. From development experts, performance coaches, and talent acquisition specialists, Clio's intentional design of its human systems is a force multiplier for the business.

Clio acknowledges that the HR function in many organizations, and especially those that have grown as they have, can roll out systems and processes that impede the agile learning and conversations that need to take place. From the beginning, as new hires started showing up every day, Clio's co-founders thought through how their human systems should develop and be managed. They wanted to create a disruptive HR organization that would staunchly avoid a heavy lift of process, and continually deploy tools that are lightweight and really serve the organization, not the back-office function that supports it. They strive to provide counterweights of process and conversation that keep problem solving and innovation at the forefront.

They also believe in evolving a process, trying it in one area or team and testing its ability to scale. Using an approach they call the MVI—the minimal viable intervention—they test out new ways of doing things; it may not be perfect, but it never holds people back. For example, if there are communication or process issues, they look for peer led solutions, not an HR driven solution. They are there to facilitate what works.

By any measure, Clio is a results-driven organization, and the Talent Team see themselves as culture ambassadors with a pulse on those times when the revenue drum beats too hard and there's a need to look at the soft balance that keeps the place and people together. "We are the accelerators of the organization. The People Innovation Lab that drives growth and culture. We are the business partner to every other department."

Beyond the company's stellar financial results, a key measure of how well their approach to performance mastery works is the degree to which people "hang out." Individuals are given autonomy on how they govern their work time, and as a result, they don't necessarily feel the compulsion to leave the physical office at a specified hour if they don't want to. The work surroundings are designed for comfort with natural light, ergonomic furnishings, common areas for collaboration or quiet reflection, beer taps, and of course, the yoga room.

"Most organizations exploit only a fraction of the knowledge, experience, and intellectual capital that is available to them. But the healthy ones tap into almost all of it. That, as much as anything else, is why they have such an advantage over their unhealthy competitors."

- Patrick Lencioni, *The Advantage*

5 Learning Management

Whether your organization employs ten, a hundred, or a thousand, your learning culture, and the learning management that supports it, is where innovation and creativity truly live. It's how the business expands its capabilities because of the accumulated know-how and know-what of your people, and how that gets shared for the benefit of the organization, customers, and the stakeholders you serve.

Why is this important? Without active and intentional learning, your people and organization will stagnate quickly, leading to declining competitiveness, lost productivity, and a failure to deliver on financial goals. The more learning is alive and well in your workplace, the stronger your learning culture will be. Let's look at its components, and how they can work together to build the intellectual capital of your business.

Most organizations offer their employees and managers some sort of compliance training, which can be considered ground zero for learning. It's compliance, after all, and making sure this training takes place ensures the organization is covering the regulations and requirements it needs to be in its sector. For example, accountants, lawyers, property managers, financial advisors, and other professionals who work in a regulated environment are required to take professional training every year to maintain their license or designation. Safety training and IT certifications are other examples. Most organizations deliver on this minimum, which represents largely informational or technical learning.

An extension of compliance training is what we call training essentials—the internal training that's delivered to teach new hires and staff about the tools, processes, and systems that are job or company specific. Typically, companies invest in some of this during the onboarding of new hires, and too often leave it at that. Companies who realize the value of ongoing training ensure everyone gets periodic refreshers, or participates in full training any time a new process is launched or a new system is rolled out.

Companies who invest time and money at the next level, that of facilitated learning, take learning deeper to build on employees' skills through targeted programs and initiatives. These are often tied to leader and manager development or other specific soft skills learning. This includes competencies such as negotiating, conflict management, strategic planning, or financial management. Learning investments are valued and people are encouraged to take the time they need to get this development. What differentiates this learning is that it's event-driven, so people take time away from their normal routines to participate. Often they're required to share key learnings with their team by way of follow-up. Facilitated learning will always have a place because it offers individuals a chance to focus solely on the topic or skill being explored and gives them the space to integrate new concepts and understanding. Importantly, it provides a setting where interacting with others helps reinforce new ideas and provides the forum for talking through the challenge of expanding one's expertise.

A continuous learning culture is really the zenith because it occurs in the real-time experiences people have at work every day. It's estimated that 70% of workplace learning comes from experience. When individuals work through situations that are first time for them or actively seek out new challenges and opportunities, continuous learning takes hold. The most vibrant learning cultures ensure this learning is conscious, meaning that learning moments are captured and acknowledged by managers as they occur. There is an expectation that individuals will discuss what they're learning whether it comes from successes, setbacks, or failures. It's also estimated that 20% of workplace learning comes from what we learn from others, including peers, subject matter experts, mentors, even customers and vendors and what we teach them. Learning from experience and learning from others can be further enhanced through educational videos, reading articles and books, listening to podcasts, Ted Talks, and the like.

What kind of learning culture does your organization have? If innovation and the successful launch of new products and services are driving your business forward, you have many opportunities to make learning management a strategic activity. In that environment, people can be "learning conscious," actively learning and sharing with others, and supporting their experience with many forms of facilitated learning. Given estimates that many technical skills one acquires today will become obsolete within two years, every organization must become a learning organization. Besides, your new hires—and younger workers in particular—expect to continue learning in real-time throughout their careers, and will leave if they don't find that kind of robust culture in your workplace.

Some Facts about Learning Management:

> Becoming obsolete is the biggest concern for today's workers, two times more concerning than the possibility of being laid off (Oxford Economics).

> Job related training and development opportunities directly influence an employee's decision to stay with a company (CED Magazine).

> Learning integration is most effective when it's delivered within the workflow, when workers can access content at the point of need from short videos and multi-media that cater to various learning styles.

> Microlearning experiences, where the learning process unfolds with short, focused content, is becoming a force multiplier for workplace learning. Estimates are that it costs 50% less overall, is 300% faster to develop, and drives 20% more learning retention (Jobenomics "The U.S. Contingent Workforce Challenge").

> Facilitated learning delivered in short episodes also enhances learning retention. The facilitator moves participants through cycles of content, delivered in various formats, with time to activate new behaviours in between. Transfer of knowledge is the focus and the metric for evaluating learning effectiveness.

> Between 2000 and 2013, the average attention span fell from twelve seconds to eight seconds—less than that of a goldfish. The age of continuous distraction has been ushered in by information overload, social media, push notifications, and a 24/7 news cycle (Microsoft Canada "Attention Spans," Consumer Insights).

> Social learning is an informal approach to learning driven by the knowledge of peers through social media, blogs, wikis, and forums that provide a range of platforms for interaction.

How Knowledge Sharing Can Be Your Competitive Advantage

A culture of knowledge sharing may be one of the most strategic levers your organization can use to drive innovation and stay competitive. How do you capture the specialized "know-how and know-what" that your tenured leaders, rising stars, and experienced technical professionals bring to work every day? Their tacit knowledge and on-the-job expertise drives business success, and you can't afford to lose what they know. Retaining and sharing intellectual capital is an essential business process.

To start, it's important to understand that knowledge transfer can encompass several types of knowledge. In related research, the Conference Board has identified three that are most critical. At the foundational

Whether you call it wisdom, experience, tribal knowledge, or just plain common sense, there are many ways to encourage, support, and make the most of knowledge sharing for yourself and your team.

level is specific knowledge, the building blocks or core tasks that make up systems, tools, and relationships. The next level is analytic knowledge, the processes, "cookbooks," frameworks, guidelines, and patterns; this is the logic that holds specific knowledge together. The third kind of knowledge is intuitive or embedded knowledge, the flow of practiced expertise in which specific and analytic knowledge becomes automatic. This is knowledge one acquires through deliberate practice and encompasses interpretation, knowing, improvisation, social, relationship, and organizational knowledge. It's the intuitive or embedded knowledge that ultimately makes up the company's intellectual property and is essential to impart to younger or less experienced individuals, emerging leaders, and subject matter or technical experts.

Workplace conversations are the primary way to discover what you know and share your knowledge, whatever that type of knowledge may be. Whether you call it wisdom, experience, tribal knowledge, or just plain common sense, there are many ways to encourage, support, and make the most of knowledge sharing for yourself and your team.

On an individual level:

If you're acquiring knowledge and learning from others, inquire while you learn. Ask, what are the most important things to learn? What's important and not so obvious? What can hurt me if I don't figure it out?" What documentation, shortcuts, or tools are especially useful? Ask why and how as much as what.

If you're offering your expertise, inquire before you share. Ask, what experiences has the person/team had with this type of task or project? How does the new task or project compare to what they already know? What do they want to learn? How do they best learn? From information, people, action, or a combination?

Above all, think twice before saying "We don't do it that way," or "We tried that and it didn't work." Ask yourself if you are perpetuating obsolete knowledge, or shutting out new ideas in favour of "it's how we've always done things."

At the team level:

In a team context, formalized knowledge sharing doesn't need to be time consuming or costly. In fact, it can facilitate skill building and lead to breakthrough thinking and innovation. Here are a few approaches to try:

- Embed in a weekly team meeting some time for each team member, including you, to share what they're going to learn and teach in the coming week. Follow up at each meeting.
- Have experts share their experience through storytelling.

- Senior leaders hold workshops or lunch 'n learns to transfer critical knowledge between tenured and emerging leaders and the team.
- Hold a facilitated retrospect session soon after project completion; embed this in your standard project management process.
- Use a knowledge capture process to post the output from the retrospect or other captured knowledge, lessons learned and good practices on the company intranet.
- Encourage younger generation talent to build blogs and use story-telling to routinely document what they are learning in their areas of interest and expertise.
- Develop and support a cross-organizational learning group to continuously, regularly share and transfer knowledge across business-critical subject areas or functions.

It's great news when people find themselves in a state of perpetual learning; some days we are the expert, other days we are the learner. When viewed through the lens of a learning partnership between teacher and learner, your company's knowledge legacy can honour the acquired intellectual capital of everyone in your workplace, regardless of age, tenure, or experience.

The Benefits of Facilitated Learning

Developing the talents and leadership skills of your people requires a multi-faceted approach. Integrating the lessons of experience can't happen without training, coaching/mentoring, and facilitated learning experiences. When it comes to workplace learning, one of the key frustrations many professionals express is that they simply do not have enough time to effectively collaborate with colleagues. The value of a shared learning experience cannot be understated.

Here are the key wins that facilitated learning offers:

- **There's life beyond your desk.** When learning as a group, professionals can't help but consider the perspectives, accomplishments, and frustrations of their colleagues.
- **In it together.** By including employees with different roles and mandates in the learning experience, you are communicating that consistency and transparency are important to you.
- **Show, don't tell.** By witnessing how mentors and senior team members receive and communicate information in the context of formal learning, standards for leadership behaviour within your organization can be set.
- **Your piece of the puzzle.** Employees feel empowered when they see that their contributions make an impact on organizational goals. Offering the experience of shared professional development facilitates this.
- **Time to streamline.** Unique formal learning situations can augment or even replace certain standard training procedures.
- **See it differently.** Allowing hard-working professionals a change of pace and an opportunity to sit back and learn for a day or a portion of a day, may ignite a creative spark in some or reinvigorate them.

Formal or facilitated learning experiences serve to bring people together. By simulating desired leadership behaviours and problem-solving approaches, they deliver insights and skill building that individuals cannot get working alone or one-on-one. They create networking opportunities and allow current and emerging leaders to see each other in action, in learning and reflecting, and sharing the lessons of experience.

How to Get ROI on Your Training Investments

Investing in the formal professional development of your team members with practical knowledge-based training or the less-tangible "soft skills" can be a costly endeavour. Time, energy, attitude, and money are all on the line. Like any investment, you want to see the returns, and too often they are hard to quantify. However, you know without training, your team simply won't function at the optimal level. Here are some suggestions to maximize the return on your training investments.

1. **Sell the Training Well.** To fully engage your staff in active participation, consider the "what's in it for me" mindset that surfaces when they are asked to take time out of their regular routines to expand their skills, thinking, or perspectives. Be creative and informal when promoting training and development programs to staff. What knowledge, insight, or skill-set will it provide them with, and how will acquiring the learning improve their work life or advance their career? Rather than sending out a dull group email scheduling everyone for a half-day "productivity software" session, consider the ways that getting up-to-speed with the new technology will allow them to solve problems more efficiently, complete projects to a higher level and help them find a greater level of success within their job. Communicate this thoughtfully, or else

the general impression will be, "My boss is trying out some new time management training, and I don't know why I'm involved."

2. **Communicate the Training Agenda in Advance.** Before the training session, distribute an outline of the key concepts that will be covered. This should be a simple but well-designed document or communication that will inspire curiosity about the subject matter, proposing questions rather than answering them. When you set people's brains up with a blueprint of what's to come, they will be more open to the concepts as they are presented. Think of venturing out for a drive in a new city. When you've had a chance to briefly glance at the map before you head out, you catalogue a general sense of the route in your brain and then, when you are actually driving and following the specific, block by block directions, you have some assurance that you're going the right way, that the distance you've travelled feels appropriate, and so on. Your confidence in your own abilities has increased since you understood the big picture before being caught up in the details.

3. **Consider Speed Training.** A recent trend is to offer learning bursts, or short, energized training sessions of 60-90 minutes. In his book *How we Learn*, science reporter Benedict Carey suggests that day-long development sessions force people to use a significant portion of brain power on simply staying attentive, thus less material is actually retained. By being efficient and faster-paced, trainers can get the vital information across in a way that is more likely to stick with participants. In extended sessions there is a tendency to let the mind wander back to the many projects and issues waiting back at one's desk. To ask your employees to leave their work behind for just an hour or two can benefit their level of learning more profoundly while making less of a dent in productivity that an all-day interruption would.

4. **Space Between Sessions.** To make your speed training sessions as effective as possible, try to schedule two of them within several days or a week or two of each other. By asking people to recall and

reconsider their learning at a second session within a few days of the first one, you'll be promoting long-term retention of the material. Sleep, rest, and distance from newly acquired information allows our subconscious to process it and acts as a "finisher," solidifying it inside the newly created pathways in our brain. By then having to review and reiterate it again in short order, we can ensure that it stays put for the long term and that we are better able to apply it to a variety of situations.

5. **Change the Learning Environment.** Researchers have also proven that our brains create new associations with the material we are learning when we are exposed to it in different situations. We are more likely to recall information that we have retained in more than one environment. Even holding one session in the open office area rather than the same old meeting room can give it a different feel.

6. **Follow up and Accountability.** The key to gaining a robust understanding of a new skill or concept is to apply it in a real-life situation. By asking participants to commit to action steps they'll take to start integrating the new learning, is one of the most powerful ways to ensure the training is being applied. Following up, either individually or at a team meeting to see what's worked and where they may be struggling, can help them share their learning experiences, and also demonstrate that you and your organization are committed to successful training outcomes. When it comes to soft-skills training, the value of some individual follow-on coaching by an internal or external coach, can make all the difference in helping even the most motivated learner take their skills to the next level.

7. **Follow Up With Expanded List of Fundamentals.** Take the bare-bones list of fundamentals that you distributed prior to the session and complete it with definitions, examples, and key concepts. Do this a week or so after the training cycle, creating reinforcement and an opportunity for your team to further engage with the content and

accommodate those with a learning style geared more toward the
written word or visual depictions.

In order to get the most of your training investments, success depends
on fostering an environment of inquiry, positivity, and informal knowledge sharing. Appreciate and encourage those who pursue new ways
to be better. Set yourself and your team up for success by approaching
necessary training with creativity and excitement and the rewards will
soon appear.

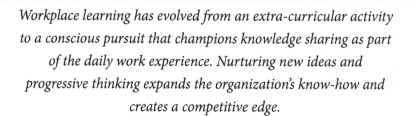

Learning Management from Basic to Brilliant

Workplace learning has evolved from an extra-curricular activity to a conscious pursuit that champions knowledge sharing as part of the daily work experience. Nurturing new ideas and progressive thinking expands the organization's know-how and creates a competitive edge.

Assess the Basics:

› Compliance training is funded, supported, and tracked by the company. Other forms of formal learning are made available based on a set budget per employee. The choice of training may or may not be company-wide, or may be a course chosen by the employee for which fees are reimbursed upon completion.

› A "buddy" system is established to facilitate new hire onboarding, though that relationship may not be formalized for continuous learning beyond ninety days.

› Lunch 'n Learns provide informal opportunities where managers or employees give short talks about what they are working on, a problem they are trying to solve, imparting new knowledge, or sharing a success story. They are a powerful forum for knowledge sharing across teams.

› Individuals learn from the experience of cleaning up a mess, fixing a troubled situation, product, system, process, or client.

› Individuals create job aids such as a flow chart, or cheat sheet, as a result of learning a piece of information, skills, or formalizing a process, and share the job aid with others.

› Individuals are encouraged to self-document repeatable processes that are a routine part of their work (such as accounting or customer service tasks), including templates and inquiry approaches used to determine decision making or next steps.

› A "lessons learned" or an "after-action" session is held after project completion or when significant milestones are reached.

› One-on-one mentoring is usually informal and occurs in real-time mentoring moments.

› Web-based and on-line courses are made available, including the sanctioned time to complete them.

› Technology is a prime medium of knowledge transfer: Instant messaging, chat room, file sharing, streaming content, web links to share favourite websites, and videos.

Accelerate with Brilliance:

- ▶ Workplace learning is intentionally woven into the daily work experience regardless of the format: peer-to-peer dialogue, online or cloud-based learning resources, or formal instructor-led sessions.

- ▶ Teams meet on a routine basis while working on a project or activity. They debrief "learning while doing" with the goal of improving performance the next day.

- ▶ Company stories are told to enhance employee understanding of what makes the business tick. For example, a video clip of how the company's products and services have made a difference, or profiling individuals or teams as they champion the company's values.

- ▶ Learning resources are easily searchable, accessible, and consumable. Above all, they are continually updated so individuals always have relevant knowledge about how the business works today.

- ▶ There are cross-functional opportunities for individuals to participate in or lead something new—a system upgrade or implementation, product launch, service enhancement, project, or way of doing things.

- ▶ Senior leaders hold seminars for the purpose of transferring critical knowledge to managers and emerging leaders.

› Cross-functional learning groups or communities of practice are established to continuously share and transfer knowledge across subject areas or functions.

› Some form of knowledge capture process is used to post lessons learned on projects or application of company best practices. This information is made accessible on the company's intranet.

› Next generation or younger employees in particular are encouraged to contribute to the company's blog and use storytelling to routinely document what they are learning in their areas of interest and expertise.

Learning Management Innovator: Vivo Team

Vivo Team is a web-based performance management solutions company founded on a deep passion and drive to create highly functioning teams in the workplace. To the company, the name Vivo means Vital, Alive, and Engaged, and their platform diagnoses, trains, and analyzes team performance to build teams and develop leaders. They bring learners together in online classrooms with live, instructor-led training with both individual and group coaching that truly delivers.

The Vivo organization is represented by a team of accomplished professionals with deep expertise in developing teams and leaders. The importance of practicing internally what they teach on learning management is part of their cultural DNA. Their team has come together from

> "By prioritizing learning within our organization, we've created a nimble team capable of achieving great things with fewer people."

across the globe and a variety of industries; they bring a diverse set of skills and international experience, allowing them to grow their own organization from a unique perspective. Their culture is built on the foundation of providing opportunities—and structures—for every team member to enhance their capabilities by managing their own learning in a number of ways. As Erin Berube, General Manager, says, "By prioritizing learning within our organization, we've created a nimble team capable of achieving great things with fewer people."

At the individual level, formal learning begins with onboarding new team members. All employees go through Vivo's training on team soft skill and leadership development, which sets them up to be productive and engaged team members with first-hand understanding of the business. From there, additional learning resources are made available, customized to meet specific needs, such as sales coaches for the sales team, on-camera training for their trainers and coaches, and key business training for their operations team.

At the organizational level, Vivo is a virtual company with a dispersed team across Canada, so their operational structure necessitates a built-in structure of collaboration and learning that's become critical to their success. Formal meeting structures incorporate:

- Weekly direct ongoing swift encounter (DOSE) meetings to celebrate wins and identify stuck points.
- A learning channel built into Slack where they share new learnings across every aspect of the business.
- A weekly meeting structure where at the end of meetings, appreciations, difficulties, and final statements are shared by each person to encourage real time learning and feedback within the team.

Positioned at the leading edge of learning innovation, Vivo's investments in the know-how of their people allows them to accelerate the evolution of their product and service offering. Learning management is the heartbeat of their exponential business growth.

"In absolute terms, challenging assignments are the best teacher. They are most likely to be remembered as development and they teach the greatest variety and the largest number of lessons."

- Mike Lombardo & Bob Eichinger, Center for Creative Leadership

6 Talent Development

We frequently get questions from leaders about the challenges of developing their people. They aren't sure what to make of a star performer who leaves after a couple of years to pursue career growth elsewhere when it appeared the individual was progressing nicely. They want to support individuals in developing their professional capabilities, but aren't sure how to get started or how to make development a thriving part of the company culture. Often there are some misunderstandings and outright myths that stand in the way of making development happen. Let's look at the most prevalent and what you can do about them:

Myth #1: Confusing training with development. Training is often about skill building and it's an essential part of development but only one part of it. Where development really happens is in the daily work experiences people have, especially when they are challenged to excel at what they do. Examples would be the need to use good judgment in setting priorities in order to meet multiple deadlines, deal with complicated customer or supplier issues, solve a production problem, sort out an accounting discrepancy—all are situations that are developmental for people. If you provide skills-based training for your people, great, but that probably counts for only 10% of their development. The rest will come from real-time experience and learning from others. If people say there's a lack of focus on their development, and you're providing some training, or only sending people to conferences, you may be missing the mark. For more on this point, see the chapter on learning management.

Myth #2: Talent development means promotions and advancement up the corporate ladder. This is a more dated view of development, where there's a hierarchy and we assume most everyone wants to get to the next rung on the ladder, the sooner the better. When most people are asked what they want from their careers or development opportunities, one of the number one responses is to use their talents creatively, to learn new tasks, get exposure to different people, and take on projects never tackled before. Most of all, they seek feedback on how they are doing. This means that most talent development is really about how people grow-in-place, or "bloom where they are planted," which is essential as the hierarchy in most small to mid-market enterprises is pretty flat and the opportunities to advance may be few. But the opportunities to develop are many.

Myth #3: Development is only for managers or aspiring leaders. This is actually a cop-out, and often turns development into management training or formal leadership development programs for the most promising emerging leaders. These individuals only make up about ten percent of your workforce, which means relegating everyone else to merely performing on the job without a clear line of sight on where the future may take them. It's reality without hope. The massive—or even lean—numbers of people in the middle are where the best opportunities are for development. Providing real-time coaching as individuals master the challenges in their work, and providing feedback on strengths and areas that can be further developed, can increase engagement across the organization. This coach approach creates a motivational environment where people want to excel and continue to grow.

Myth #4: We're so busy there's no time to focus on development. This is another abdication of responsibility as managers rationalize their way out of the development imperative. Often development planning or the very thought of it conjures up images of forms, complicated goal setting, checklists, documentation, deadlines, and promises of promotions or the requirement to have an answer for where an individual's future may be.

While some documentation is helpful to ensure agreement on goals and direction and facilitates timely follow up, the reality is most development planning happens in conversations. It's the quality of a conversation that matters most to individuals; the opportunity to meet with their managers at least a couple of times a year to talk about their strengths, what's working for them at work, what could be better, and what could be done to increase their value to the organization while supporting their professional interests. These conversations don't have to be lengthy summits, and several twenty-minute conversations over a period of many months can have a lot more impact than one annual stress-filled event. You get more points for stimulating thinking than for how long the conversation is. The outcome—real development—can show up in small, subtle ways that over time create greater challenge, interest, and satisfaction at work.

If you're daunted by the challenge of developing your people, consider reframing your understanding of what it means, how it works, and what it takes to make it happen. The reality is development is a daily occurrence in your workplace whether you're aware of it or not. The opportunities lie in conversations, a higher level of awareness, and the responsibility that both managers and team members have to chart the course to cut through the clutter and figure out what employees really need.

Some Facts about Talent Development:

> Lack of growth opportunities is one of the biggest reasons employees seek out new positions outside their current employer.

> People who are gaining the skills and experiences they need to reach their career goals are seven times more likely to be highly engaged than those who are not. Conversely, people without career-growth opportunities are thirteen times more likely to disengage at work than those who have such opportunities (Deloitte Bersins research).

> Across industries, it takes people on average twelve years to move from an entry-level position to rank of supervisor or above. This most often consists of having four to five jobs at three or four different employers and four different job titles (Stats Canada).

> Up to 88% of people have to change companies to obtain a position of greater responsibility (Workopolis research).

> The most important methods to retain support staff are stretch assignments, professional development, and job rotations. For professionals, it's transparency around internal career opportunities, professional development, and short-term assignments in other areas of the company (Human Capital Institute Research).

> According to the Business Family Centre at UBC's Sauder School of Business, only 30% of businesses successfully make the transition

to the next generation of family leadership. At the same time, 90% of them expect to transition leadership to a family member (Family Enterprise Exchange).

> Individuals who are successful developmentally are more likely to have active and numerous learning strategies, which help them learn what to do when they don't know what to do.

The Challenge of "Career"

Many companies continuously receive low marks for career opportunities on employee surveys. Recent career development research indicates that the issue is far more complex than providing career paths or more jobs, which is challenging enough in the small to mid-size enterprise. Most employees, unfortunately, don't have clarity around their career aspirations or drivers of job satisfaction. That's their problem, not their employer's—until they leave to pursue a vague, often unfounded notion of a promising career move.

Another factor at play is that despite widespread misunderstandings of what a career actually looks like and the efforts of organizations to educate employees on today's career landscape (such as lateral moves, special assignments, development "in place"—not just promotions), engagement surveys and the language of many managers tends to reinforce yesterday's language of advancement and career. A career does not have to be defined by a progressive pathway that ticks appropriate boxes. By providing learning opportunities and encouraging employees to build networks and develop relationships, you can help to shift people's traditional views of career to something uniquely personal. A career is determined by an individual's choices, and a good employer will observe and support those choices. Perhaps it's time to evolve the definition of a career by asking people if their choice would be to have a future with their organization.

Why the Newly Promoted Don't Always Deliver on their Promise

Developing and promoting internal talent is essential to building a strong, sustainable organization. Whether the advancement of a fast track star is in play, or the long-awaited promotion of a stellar high performer, offering these cherished opportunities for recognition and development are key to retaining top talent and the successful pursuit of business goals. It can be disappointing and surprising though, that once in their new positions, these capable individuals don't always deliver on their promise. It seems everything was aligned: the individual has received great mentoring and coaching, is well regarded by others, and had a variety of experiences and yet, somehow their fit in a leadership role is underwhelming, or worse, an utter failure. What's happened here?

In working with leaders to help them make the best selection and development decisions, they often present a number of characteristics or behaviours as criteria for advancement. These leadership criteria can include the ability to provide the appropriate level of guidance and direction to their team members, adjust their communication style to meet various situations, recognize the need for change when it's needed, and make timely decisions after considering multiple perspectives.

The thing is that those characteristics, and others like them, aren't always inherent within strong individual contributors, and when undeveloped, lead to struggle when the newly promoted are faced with the demands of a leadership role. Most of us know someone who was promoted out of a job they were great at, only to struggle with their new responsibilities. When this happens, there is a failure on the organization's part to recognize the significant differences between contributor and leadership roles. What's needed here is a more robust approach to assessment that goes beyond strong performance in the current role.

Let's look at a few recent examples where these situations could have been avoided if a more robust assessment of the individual had taken place before promotion was considered.

Blair is hard-working, task focused, and team-oriented. His work as a maintenance technician at a heavy equipment manufacturer was terrific. His colleagues loved working with him, his performance was always rated at the top of his group, and his manager had tapped him for promotion.

However, Blair did not like to take responsibility or control over the actions of others. He was most comfortable working within a group where the direction and activities were determined by others. When he was brought into an acting manager role, he struggled to provide the necessary supervision and guidance to his team. When asked by junior maintenance staff for guidance on simple tasks that he was an expert in, he would gather the group together to reach consensus on what should be done.

Tamara too is hard working, personable, and seeks out predictability, consistency, clear expectations, and processes. As an HR specialist, her can-do attitude and knowledge of guidelines and processes made her a star in her organization. Tamara's friendliness and empathy made her easily approachable and a favourite employee to work with. Given her effectiveness, she was also identified as leadership material. However, her desire to establish close relationships with employees made it difficult for her to make tough decisions. As well, her reliance on guidelines and processes became a problem at the managerial level where the willingness to consider new ideas and approaches was required.

Then there was Braden, a driven and ambitious individual who was innovative, enjoyed challenges, and was incredibly bright. His work as an electrical engineer was highly regarded, and he had been given a number of high profile projects to work on, with great success. When given a team leader position, Braden struggled for the first time in his career. While he was comfortable telling people what to do, he was much less effective at mobilizing people around a purpose. Members of his group complained about being treated like minions, and the productivity of the team fell dramatically.

Each of these professionals—Blair, Tamara, and Braden—can and did do good work, but each had struggles moving into leadership roles.

The next time your organization is looking to move a solid performer into a leadership role, clarify first what their new position will demand and what is needed for them to be successful as a leader, not what has made them successful so far.

These struggles are quite common, and can be identified early in someone's leadership career well before they burn bridges, negatively impact organizational performance, or leave because of a poor fit.

A robust process of assessment can provide critical information regarding an individual's readiness for leadership and ensure that promotional decisions aren't made solely based on stellar performance or knowledge of the business. It should consider assessments of cognitive ability, personality fit with the team, aspiration, alignment with corporate goals and values, and situational judgment. These measures help identify the leadership strengths and development priorities in an objective and valid way. The initial effort put into taking such an in-depth look is important because the impact of poor leadership is so significant.

The next time your organization is looking to move a solid performer into a leadership role, clarify first what their new position will demand and what is needed for them to be successful as a leader, not what has made them successful so far. These are often very different things. If the individual isn't ready for a formal leadership role, it doesn't mean they won't ever be. It will be necessary to position them for the development they need, or ensure they continue to enjoy roles and responsibilities that truly are a good fit for them and the business.

Your People Need Development Plans. Here's How to Get Started.

When we talk of development plans, sometimes the very words conjure visions of employee weakness or problem, and not necessarily a path forward for positive improvement. Too often, development has a deficit-based tone to it, resulting in weak enthusiasm for the whole planning process. In addition, "development" activities, when they do happen, become an add-on to an employee's existing workload instead of an experience embedded in their day-to-day responsibilities.

How do you create a development plan, or make development happen in a way that engages the individual in the process, delivers the experiences and support they need to grow, and provides the platform for even further growth?

Powerful development plans are focused on the present as well as the future and include creative ways to use the current job as a learning lab. The actions included in an effective plan are meaningful and the anticipated outcomes compelling enough to make development an ongoing priority.

Modern, holistic development plans incorporate three elements.

Experience: The majority of development occurs through experience: challenging tasks, assignments, and projects. In conversation with their managers, individuals must understand what they need to know, or improve on, and construct an assignment that forces them to get their feet wet. Examples of stretch experiences include presenting a report to management, launching a process change, or leading a team in a branch office.

Exposure: The second element is learning from others, or the exposure, that comes from interactions with others in the course of completing tasks and projects. Think of a skill your employee needs to further hone or even learn from scratch. Think of someone who demonstrates that skill effortlessly and watch them in action. Examples of development from exposure include chairing a staff meeting, making a key hiring decision, working in another unit for a short time, or leading a team in an area where one is an expert.

Education: The third element is formal learning like courses, webinars, books, and facilitated learning experiences. Too often, development is considered just about training and formal courses, and while that's an important part of it, the best leverage of formal learning comes from its integration (testing and applying concepts) in the context of ongoing experiences and exposure to others one can learn from. It's estimated that formal learning counts for 10 to 25% of workplace learning.

Creating the plan is one exercise, but what makes development really happen are the conversations that take place between the manager and employee. If development conversations happen annually, they become a one-and-done activity, with a checklist and form completed. Today, when employees want more frequent and informal conversations about development and growth, it's important to break the annual cycle by weaving development into the fabric of the employee's work itself, as described above, with the manager taking advantage of common interactions that surround those activities. Those common interactions can include questions to prompt reflection about what's being learned, key take-aways, and what might be done differently next time.

Founders Need Development Too

Daniel is the founder and CEO of what has been a successful and profit-able company by most measures; it has an enviable twenty-year history, products, and services that have been in demand, a stellar customer list, and for the most part, a loyal team of managers and employees. In the last few years, he's noticed that growth has stalled, different from the nor-mal ups and downs he's experienced in the past. To compound this, his management team is not as engaged as it was, and in the last six months, three key customers have moved on to a competitor. While Daniel looks at his team and the marketplace for insights into his next steps, he might consider whether he's become a victim of his own success. Ironically, he may have failed to develop his leadership potential. When this happens, a dynamic called founder's syndrome may be at play.

What is founder's syndrome? It can best be described as a predicament where a founder, once driven and decisive, becomes stagnant, languishing in his or her own success. Subtly, slowly, over time, that once-vibrant founder simply stops seeking feedback or becomes resistant to outside perspectives regarding his or her leadership. Decision making may still be the responsibility of the founder, so the same problems return to the organization over and over again, and the team struggles through, from one crisis to the next. It's possible that the founder has become impatient and defensive, blaming others for the constant complications. In turn, many direct reports do not assert themselves the way they used to, as they fear reprisal from the leader. Ideas stop bubbling up, contribution lessens, and innovation stops.

It's important to know that founder's syndrome isn't necessarily about the actual founder of an organization. The central figure could be the person who succeeded the founder, or an individual who assumed respon-sibility during a time of crisis and led the business into clearer waters. Sometimes, it's just the person who has been at the helm for too long.

Founder's syndrome often affects the small to mid-size enterprise during one (or both) of the following two phases. The first is during the transition from entrepreneurial, breakneck speed, and chaotic growth, to sustainable, stable, well-planned, and managed development. The second

> **Leaders of lasting, well-developed organizations are courageous in governing through the business life cycle, and can develop and improve their businesses and themselves along the way.**

is from the well-managed, properly resourced, functioning business to the inevitable stage where renewal and revitalization are necessary to keep the company thriving. When founders or extremely tenured leaders don't mindfully navigate these business life-cycle transitions, the company is managed through the personality of the founder or leader, rather than by a strategic vision aimed at providing the best products or services and supporting the growth and development of individuals within the firm.

Leaders of lasting, well-developed organizations are courageous in governing through the business life cycle, and can develop and improve their businesses and themselves along the way. We've watched many great companies flourish under proactive founders, committed to charting a course that made way for others to assume control, ensuring long term success and relevance for the organization. We've also seen companies tumble because founders and senior leaders resisted calls for change or innovation and were reluctant to identify and nurture successors to shepherd the company through the next phase of its evolution.

As a leader, what can you do to prevent founder's syndrome and ensure that you can grow yourself while growing your business to its full market potential? The remedies are many:

- Acknowledge that over time, you'll need to move on or back away from daily involvement in the business. You can't be there in the same way forever, and you never know when that change will occur. Create a succession plan that will proactively ensure the viability of the organization whether you're there or not.

- Accept that another leader or leadership team will introduce changes you may not have been prepared to make. This is as it should be and is not a reflection of your earlier gift of transforming a dream into reality.
- Secure a mentor, board of directors, or advisors and an advocate from within. Founder's syndrome comes from doing what's natural for you. Changing your leadership approach after so many years may be rather unnatural. Seek and accept help.

When leaders stay on for the good of the organization, they may be orchestrating certain decline for the business. As a founder, owner, CEO, or leader, your ongoing development is essential to the lifeblood of the organization, whether you're in ascendancy, riding high, or preparing your exit strategy.

The Bottom Line Benefits of Developing Next Generation Leaders

When it comes to developing future leaders, small to mid-size enterprises can be especially challenged to dedicate the resources needed to ensure leadership continuity well into the future. At the same time, getting your ducks in a row on next generation leadership can reap significant bottom-line benefits to your organization, your business, and your customers.

The real-world nightmare is losing key leaders at the very time when their expertise, perspectives, and contemporary approaches are more important than ever. This can be the true cost of a weak process, or doing nothing at all. This happens when emerging or potential leaders don't get the support they need, or don't have a clear line of sight on what their future may look like with the organization, even in broad terms. At the same time, more tenured leaders may be denying the inevitable need to plan for their eventual departure, resisting the effort required to create a plan for stepping aside so others can step up. There are significant costs associated with turnover, and most organizations are eager to avoid that pain.

Similarly, for many smaller organizations, there may be a need to recruit future leadership talent externally. Putting off this exercise until a key person leaves, or is forced to leave for unforeseen reasons, can mean lost time and opportunity as a result of chronic leadership gaps that may be hurting the long-term health of the business.

When companies allow uncertainty and reluctance to prevail, when they don't get intentional about what the next phase of leadership will look like, they lose out on several bottom-line benefits. Three of the key ones are:

- **Better business planning.** Learning and leadership development lays the ground work for seamless leadership transition when the need arises. When organizations know they have the right people in the queue for key positions, they are better equipped to plan for business growth and expansion. This provides emerging leaders with more avenues to model diverse thinking and bring forward innovative ideas.

- **Improved retention and lower turnover.** Sound leadership development helps to ensure that employees know they're being groomed for a particular position, which gives them a strong sense of having a clearly defined future within the company. This is a strong retention tool that keeps people on a continuous learning curve, making them less reluctant to leave for greener pastures. The resulting cost savings can be substantial, even though an upfront investment of time and money is essential.

- **Increased levels of employee engagement and contribution.** Working with potential or emerging leaders to create a learning plan shows trust and asks individuals to step up and stretch themselves. This can be a powerful motivational tool. If they know that a path with an upward career trajectory exists within the organization, they may be willing to make a greater commitment to the business.

It's a common occurrence for once-profitable companies to suffer significant losses, both the financial and human kind, when concrete succession plans are not in place and a leadership change looms. Reasons for avoiding this kind of future-proofing are diverse, but in our experience, are often about current leaders being too busy, too distracted, or simply blind to the possibility that change may come about sooner than they expect. Yet forecasts suggest that many mid-sized companies will be losing 30-50 % of their leaders over the next three years. Business owners and executives need to make time for the strategic thinking required to identify and prepare emerging leaders. The future health of any successful business depends on it.

How to See the Light in Succession Planning

Succession planning is an essential business process in need of a rethink and recalibration. For small businesses and larger organizations alike to reap the benefits of this evolving human system, the time has come to go beyond the traditional and often singular focus on founder, CEO, or senior leadership succession. From our experience, seeing the light is reached when succession planning merges talent planning and development, and encompasses critical roles, top talent, and emerging high performers at every level across the enterprise.

Planning for successors—not just in the C-suite, but in all positions crucial to an organization's ability to execute strategy—provides vital support for overall business performance. Ensuring key positions are filled with qualified individuals who are highly skilled in what they do makes for a strong business foundation and continuity in management. In turn, a solid and dependable structure within leadership and other essential positions adds to an organization's effort to deploy its financial and human resources effectively. Such stability makes a positive contribution to overall talent management: recruitment, retention, talent development, and employee engagement. Absent an effective succession planning effort, a business stands to lose a great deal.

The following five pathways pave the road to success:

1. Refreshed and revisited role definitions should be in place for critical roles before any assessment can take place of either internal or external leadership successors. Looking at what will be required to successfully lead the organization into the future may be very different from what it's taken to get the business to where it is today. The structure

of the management team going forward may need to be revisited to accommodate new business realities and the developing competencies of current and emerging leaders.

2. Shifting business strategies can mean new roles become critical to business success. A new emphasis on a specific product or service offering may mean that positions and roles related to the go-to-market efforts for that offering should now be included in the formal succession or talent planning process. A clear view into the competencies and requirements for these newly critical roles is essential to start this effort.

3. Retaining your key players long enough for them to take on roles of greater responsibility can be a challenge with the mobility of today's workforce. Typically, your rising stars are looking for ongoing development opportunities, so creating experiences that involve internal moves can go a long way to maximize their current skills and expand their competencies in new areas. This may include a scope change such as setting up a branch office or other meaty assignments where they will be pushed to produce in settings or with challenges they haven't experienced before. Provide mentors and frequent feedback to remind them continually of the importance of their contributions—and their development.

4. Invest in proactive efforts to replace the talent you may lose. For critical positions, consider ramping up recruiting efforts to connect with talented individuals with the right mix of skills who may be considered future team members. While most companies think only of internal talent for succession planning, adding external talent (candidates) to succession plans increases the number of potential successors.

5. When no leadership successor is apparent, the recruitment and integration of external talent will be necessary to ensure continuity of the business. Bringing in a senior leader from outside can be a recipe for disaster when the cultural integration doesn't go well; however, with

the right planning and assessment of key leadership roles and what the ideal candidates need to bring, this important step can and has been successfully accomplished in many small to mid-size enterprises and large organizations alike.

Done well, these steps will realize a return on investment that pays off handsomely when succession moves need to happen. The process itself serves to support a foundation for organizational renewal and a re-commitment of current leaders to developing and advancing talent as a lever in achieving business goals. The recalibration can make succession planning a bright light for your organization, a vital human system that embraces talent risk management, sustainability, and the drive for business growth.

Talent Development from Basic to Brilliant

Talent planning and development is an active pursuit. It encompasses critical roles and building leaders at all levels. Professional development is planned and career growth happens even if promotional opportunities are limited and the future is uncertain.

Assess the Basics:

➤ Development is often associated with training and funding courses to support individuals in improving their technical or managerial skills.

➤ Development planning or goal setting, when it does happen, is often discussed at the same time as the performance review.

➤ While managers may help their direct reports set goals for expanded experiences and learning, it's usually in the context of enhancing performance in the current job, rather than with an eye on the future.

➤ Individuals are given opportunities to work on projects or task forces that are generally short-term, one-time events, lasting from a few months to one year.

➤ Managers may be reluctant to talk with individuals about their development as they feel they need to have an answer to what the future might hold and the path an individual should take to get there.

> When few or no promotional opportunities exist, development and growth is limited.

> There is little job movement between departments. Even when individuals may have transferable skills and express an interest in making a change, the tendency is to fill a role with an external hire.

> Career advancement is viewed primarily as making a move up the organizational ladder into management positions.

> Volunteer activities or participation in community events offer opportunities for individuals to develop leadership skills.

Accelerate with Brilliance:

- ‣ Managers are actively involved in talent planning, informed by an understanding of business strategy and alignment of the career aspirations and concerns of their team members.

- ‣ Career conversations are a regular part of the manager/employee dialogue.

- ‣ Career growth is supported at every level through stretch assignments, challenging projects, job moves, promotions, and enrichment opportunities.

- ‣ Managers don't assume that what they knew six months ago about the career aspirations or development needs of their people remains true today.

- ‣ Managers take the time to offer their direct reports perspective, feedback, and an organizational view of an individual's reputation.

- ‣ Managers discuss industry trends and how they relate to the competencies individuals and teams will need in the future.

- ‣ Managers connect team members to mentors, truth tellers, advocates, more senior leaders or associates in other departments/divisions, or external contacts.

> Emerging leaders are encouraged to take on or participate in assignments that require holistic thinking, the ability to see the big picture, and make decisions accordingly.

> Job shadowing is formalized to enhance cross-functional knowledge. Individuals shadow an expert or employee working in another function or department, and then debrief observations and insights with their manager.

> External peer mentoring groups are made available to emerging leaders and managers with the understanding that learning from outside experts and industry peers broadens perspectives and increases one's value to the business.

> It's understood that sometimes the organization isn't able to provide the development people seek and they may need to leave. This is not seen as a failure, rather a potential opportunity for the employee to return later with a more advanced skill set.

> When individuals have retirement on the horizon, an open conversation on transition planning takes place to ensure adequate preparation of successor(s) and thoughtful management of the departure process.

Talent Development Innovator: TimberWest Forest Products

An Innovative Approach to Succession Management and Transition Agreements

TimberWest Forest Corporation is a mid-market, privately held forest service company with operations on Vancouver Island and the BC Coast for over a hundred years. The corporate organization employs approximately 125 people, and through their contracts and managed lands, they provide thousands of direct and indirect jobs annually across coastal BC communities. They are widely recognized for managing their lands sustainably while preserving biodiversity to ensure their working forests remain healthy and productive for future generations.

The company's long-term success can be attributed to the talent of their people across head office, remote locations, and field operations. Highly skilled and experienced foresters, biologists, and technicians are mission critical to their talent base. As a progressive employer, the company has enjoyed the long tenure of many of their professionals and

> "As you can imagine, we have lots of good conversations around career—developments, changes, and succession opportunities. Some discussions end with a plan, but other people are reluctant to commit. Either way, we like to think the dialogue is fruitful and healthy."

managers. However, in the last three years, changes in executive leadership have coincided with at least a 30% turnover (10% per year) solely due to retirements. TimberWest is a flat/lean organization, so managing demographic challenges and the departure of the know-how and know-what of their tenured staff is particularly challenging when few promotional opportunities are available for emerging leaders.

The current executive leadership team is addressing this issue in part by first setting a tone of open dialogue in all employee interactions. This is considered not only essential to success, but essential to succession of the business. As a result, transition discussions are taking place regularly with their senior level people (or high professionals in unique single matter expert (SME) roles). As Jan Marston, their VP of HR says, "As you can imagine, we have lots of good conversations around career—developments, changes, and succession opportunities. Some discussions end with a plan, but other people are reluctant to commit. Either way, we like to think the dialogue is fruitful and healthy."

The intent of the transition conversations is to ensure that by the time the last year of the individual's tenure begins, there is a fully mapped transition process with key success metrics that not only create accountability, but form the basis of the individual's compensation during the transition period.

As that last year approaches, the wheels are set in motion to craft a formalized retirement transition plan. A meeting is held with the senior leader of the employee's area and the employee/manager to work through various scenarios and practical ways to structure the basics of the employment structure during the transition. The work arrangements may change if the employee/manager wants that and the company is able to accommodate. For example, transition to a reduced workweek can be a common transition request, and the impact on company policies, benefits, and CRA compliance must be considered in mapping out an agreement that works for both sides.

One example is a transition plan created for a highly valued subject matter expert who expressed a value on additional flexibility around hours of work, which was feasible. The plan was outlined in a manner that the company would benefit from approximately 50% of his time over the year, but if the opportunity wasn't a good fit, they could agree to accelerate the time/term of the exit.

The spirit of the conversations and resulting agreement is embedded in a desire to see someone fully engaged and giving themselves every opportunity to be a role model (or leave a legacy of sorts) so the company doesn't want to extend the individual's time to transition and have them feel the lame duck syndrome. To that end, the agreements have a few controls or checks and balances. If the work and transition plan is completed, a shorter end date can be set. If that were to happen, it is usually because someone has (a) worked hard to get their legacy knowledge passed on or (b) they have had an emotional epiphany and know they want to end their corporate chapter in life and perhaps go travel or be with family.

Delivering on key milestones and ensuring the flow of knowledge required to get one's successor(s) fully up to speed is a core requirement, and a significant portion of a variable pay bonus depended on this deliverable. Two or three performance metrics form the basis of the transition agreement. Thirty percent of the time will be spent in the field with at

Systematizing as much of their knowledge as possible, and making their transition mandate explicit to all parties is essential.

least one individual who will either directly succeed them or benefit the most of learning from them. Thirty percent of the time is to be spent documenting their business cases, history, and analytics, and another 30% is to be spent introducing successors or direct reports to their networks of industry professionals or technical resources who can help them stay ahead of the learning curve. The remaining 10% is orderly transition of their current responsibilities.

President and CEO Jeff Zweig believes that businesses are too often caught in the"institutional knowledge conundrum" where there is a hesitancy to help their high professionals move on so they hang on to them longer than they otherwise would. Systematizing as much of their knowledge as possible, and making their transition mandate explicit to all parties is essential. "We find these arrangements work well if both parties are open and transparent in their desires, and ultimately well aligned on what both parties need to be successful."

Most transition agreements are one year, though some have been extended beyond that. Their lessons learned are that one year, or even less, is ideal. The world moves faster with each passing day, providing opportunities for the next group of high potential career oriented employees to learn and accelerate their own succession capabilities as they move into a broader or promotional role. Their experience has been that the person to whom the baton is passed is often much readier for the opportunity than the supervisor or the organization gives them credit for.

"Human beings have an innate inner drive to be autonomous, self-determined, and connected to one another. And when that drive is liberated, people achieve more and live richer lives."

- Daniel H. Pink, *Drive: The Surprising Truth About What Motivates Us*

7 Re-Recruit

Businesses that thrive over the long term and manage to keep their talented people clearly have the right ingredients for high levels of engagement. In high performing organizations where people feel valued and know their work is making a difference, they are able to answer positively and without hesitancy the question, "What keeps me here?" The way employees are treated, the workplace culture, and manager/staff relationships all contribute to re-recruiting individuals in the organization's mission and the work they do every day.

We've all heard about the importance of a highly engaged workforce to productivity and competitiveness. The term "employee engagement" has had so much buzz in recent years that it's on the verge of becoming something of a cliché. As workplaces change and develop, the definition of "engagement" needs to be revised to reflect engagement over the long term—*sustainable* engagement. That includes the following three dimensions:

- **Effort:** Specifically discretionary effort. This is demonstrated when employees exhibit behaviour that goes above the basics to get the job done. Examples include enthusiasm and interest, going the extra mile for the customer, creative problem solving, and working effectively within the team.
- **Enablement:** An employee's need to be set up for success or to excel. This is where access to and interest in professional development, opportunities to cross-train and avenues for advancement come into play. A workplace culture that embraces recognition and long-term career planning supports and promotes enablement among its staff.
- **Energy:** The capacity for an employee to maintain their efforts over time. Often discretionary effort exists at the beginning of an employee's term of employment. The real test comes when boredom or complacency set in. Variety, challenge, and consistent feedback, as well as a feeling of connection to an organization and its people, provide the roots from which this energy can grow.

The combination of the three is the holy trinity that creates *sustainable* employee engagement, i.e. a significant performance advantage for your employees and for your organization.

The statistics bear this out. In a recent study by Towers Watson, Canadian companies lose an average of 8.8 days annually to "presenteeism" (lost productivity at work) for employees with high sustainable engagement, and 17.78 days per year for the disengaged. When it comes to absenteeism, their studies show that companies lose an average of three days per year for employees with high sustainable engagement, compared to nearly six days for the disengaged.

How does that translate to the bottom line? When comparing engagement data with the specific financial results of fifty global organizations, those with the highest level of sustainable engagement are on average, three times more profitable than those with low levels of engagement.

Towers Watson also estimates from their exhaustive studies that only 33% of Canadian workers are sustainably engaged. The good news is that an additional 24% of workers are considered unsupported—engaged, but not enabled to perform at a high level due to organizational barriers. This presents a huge opportunity for employers everywhere to address whatever productivity issues are present, and take the actions needed to create sustainable engagement.

One place to start is an organizational review that identifies the tensions, inconsistencies, and oversights that could be leading to employee disengagement or talent loss. Once you have that data in front of you, some possible action steps will emerge. At the heart of strong organizational cultures are moderate to high levels of engagement within a company's core ownership, leadership, or management team. Additionally, leaders must truly have an understanding of what an engaged employee looks like within *their* organization, and what factors have contributed to their commitment. Assumptions are easy to make in this regard as most everyone, whether leader or individual contributor, has felt engaged or disengaged in something at some point. Re-recruiting yourself, your leaders, and your team members requires an ongoing and verified understanding of what may be changing that can either positively or negatively affect workplace wellness and the satisfaction of everyone who works there.

Some Facts about Re-Recruit:

- › Research consistently indicates that money is not the most important factor in engaging and retaining people. When asked what keeps them, people want recognition for work well done, opportunities to learn and grow, and to be part of a great team.

- › Two-thirds of Canadian baby boomers entered their fifties in long-time employment, holding down the same job for at least twelve years. More than half worked for the same organization for twenty years or more (Stats Canada).

- › Today, only 30% of people at any level hold a job for more than four years. Millennials on average hold a job 2.7 years. Gen-Xers on average hold a job 3.4 years (Workopolis research).

- › Promotions lead to employee longevity. People who advance to a high level will stay with that organization for an average of 7.5 years, or 200% longer than the majority who do not receive promotions (Stats Canada).

- › Not feeling valued or recognized is a significant contributor to disengagement and employee departures.

- › A manager's ability to recognize and reward achievement effectively can increase an individual's discretionary effort by as much as 23%, and their intent to stay by up to 32% (Corporate Leadership Council).

> Employee retention and company culture are self-perpetuating. The stronger and more positive the culture, the less likely people are to leave, and the more people stay, the stronger the culture becomes.

> The more supportive the manager-employee relationship, the longer an individual will stay and the more favourably the individual will regard the organization after departure.

> Long-time job assignments don't have to lead to disengagement. Participation opportunities such as working groups, offsite meetings, project teams, or mentoring others can enhance enjoyment and contribution over the long term.

Why Your Corporate Values Matter More than Ever

In a world of constant change, how do you know if your organization is charting the right course to living its strategic intent and fulfilling its mission and business goals? Beyond financial results, there are other anchors that tell us how healthy an organization is and therefore how ably it delivers on its promise. Commonly understood as corporate values, these anchors represent the behaviours and beliefs that underline the work people do and how they interact with their client base and with each other. More than platitudes on a wall, when clearly identified and communicated, corporate values drive behaviour and results, and offer direction to individuals when situations require judgment calls, regardless of the situation they face.

Today, corporate values are more important than ever for three reasons:

- Many organizations across Canada are in growth mode, and growth often brings significant changes to organizational charts, workloads, and manager and team expectations. Values are the anchor that keeps people on the same page, and are particularly important to champion during transformational change. "The way we do things around here" may evolve to adapt to growth, but the corporate behaviours and beliefs help people stay the course with wisdom and integrity.
- In a marketplace where it's increasingly difficult to attract, hire, and retain great talent, corporate values can be a differentiator in attracting the right people. When clearly explained on your organization's website, they convey to potential recruits what your organization stands for and whether there's a culture match for them.
- In a time where exponential change is now the new world order, from global political shifts to economic and industry changes, people are looking for the port in the storm, and corporate values can provide the assurance that where people work and what they do is important

and really matters. When teams have shared corporate values, they have the compass for making decisions that are aligned with business direction, regardless of the external noise that filters through the workplace on a daily basis.

Here are four ways to ensure your corporate values are alive and well:

1. If your organization hasn't articulated its corporate values, it's a worthwhile exercise that brings together various perceptions of what drives behaviour and decision-making. If the values have been defined, but aren't all that compelling, now is a good time to review and refresh. Sometimes a few wording adjustments can bring new life to traditional values that may have been created years ago. Three-to-five word statements that are manageable and memorable make it easy for people to get behind. For example, if "doing the right thing" is a corporate value, then the value statement should explain how you follow through on commitments and do what you can to protect your reputation. Or, if your organization is a leader in product development, a corporate value may state something about innovation that goes beyond what's expected.

2. Can everyone articulate the corporate values and what that means for the work they do and the service they deliver, internally and externally? If collaborative work relationships are a corporate value, what does that mean for how problems are solved and decisions made? The more people understand how the values apply to what they do every day, and to the customer experience, the easier it is for them to demonstrate behaviour that's aligned with the team and culture. At weekly meetings, share stories of team members who've done a great job of exemplifying one of the corporate values. Or, consider giving periodic rewards or specific recognition for individuals who best exemplify them.

3. Make them visible. Are the values posted in meeting rooms, the office kitchen, on your website? Perhaps the way they are presented could be refreshed with a more current look. Keeping values visible reminds everyone of what the organization stands for and ensures communication both internally and externally to visitors who enter your workplace and visit your website.

4. If corporate values aren't used as part of your hiring process, start incorporating interview questions to explore the values fit with potential candidates. Do candidates demonstrate behaviours that reflect your team's values set? One of the biggest reasons for a hiring mismatch can occur when values aren't aligned. Stepping up this part of your selection process can make a difference.

Corporate values are the cornerstone of organizational culture and guide all aspects of your business, from how decisions are made and business is pursued, to whom you hire and how you reward, coach, and develop your people. In a world of ongoing change and uncertainty, make sure you're using this important lever to keep your business and people aligned with meaning and purpose.

Is Your "Fast Track" Star a Flight Risk?

The promise of promotion or eventual succession can keep your high-flying employees committed, engaged, and on the payroll, for a while. These transitions take time, especially when they are part of a long-term business growth strategy. While they wait, your people may get nervous or restless. How do you hang on to those star employees that you're grooming for more senior positions when the attractive alternatives and competing offers come knocking?

Strategies for keeping your most promising employees:

1. Through frank, ongoing conversations, continually assess your star employee's current level of engagement and commitment to staying. Be clear with your intentions for them and describe why you see them as a long-term fit for the organization.

2. Your fast track talent are above all achievement oriented, and are always interested in the next goal or milestone they need to reach. Include learning objectives along with business results when setting goals to ensure they are broadly focused on what they are doing on a daily basis, not just striving for the next sale or project completion. Learning objectives can include doing a presentation to management or a key customer, an analysis of a new product or market potential, or leading a team on a corporate initiative. Whatever the learning objective, make it a stretch objective that challenges their technical, business, and interpersonal or managerial skills.

3. Fast trackers also like to learn and share with others, so make sure they have opportunities for input, collaboration, or consultation that are cross-functional. A territorial environment won't retain your stars; they need interaction and exposure to as many areas of your organization as possible. The more connected and aligned they feel, the longer they'll stay.

4. Help them understand their impact. Whether they appreciate it or not, they are developing a reputation, or personal brand, and they need to understand how their actions and inactions contribute to how they are viewed by others. This will ultimately have weight when it comes to promotional decisions. Are they viewed as too task oriented and not focused enough on relationships? Or too conversational when a more direct approach would be warranted? If there are blind spots here, the sooner they know about it and understand the impact, the sooner a course correction can be made.

5. Timing is not always perfect for promoting your star. It's not always possible for them to achieve a milestone or reach a particular stage in their development, when an advancement opportunity comes available. With the right kinds of support, offering the next step may be a great way to test their readiness. There is always a risk to this, but time and again, we've seen that promoting high-fliers early, with a focus on fast track development, can save a company the struggle of losing their stars to competitors.

The cost of losing a great employee is significant. When you spot someone with the kind of potential and promise who you know can add value in the long-term, don't be afraid to talk to them about it, get them on board and support them in becoming the manager and leader you envision them to be. It is a risk to sit back and hope that they are engaged enough to wait patiently for an advancement opportunity. Try the approaches listed above to ensure that you don't lose your best people when a few well-executed strategies can keep them engaged and on track.

Which Millennials Are We Trying To Engage?

The expectations and motivations of millennials can be very different, depending on which end of the generation they come from. Leading edge millennials are now in their mid-thirties and many are either already in, or being considered for, managerial roles. Younger millennials are in their early to mid-twenties and have had significantly different formative experiences than their older counterparts. While older millennials began their careers during the era of "you can be anything you want to be," the younger group reached adulthood right around the 2008 global financial crisis, when jobs were few and far between. Instead of being told to "reach for the stars" this group was encouraged be practical, go where the jobs are, and get a foot in the door. What impact has this had on workplace relationships between older and younger millennials and their colleagues?

In our experience, there can be a considerable disconnect between the two groups. Operational stereotypes can cause people to disregard the differences among any given generation. Let's look at some of the key areas where you may notice distinctions between the older and the younger millennials.

The 22-29 year olds aren't just digital natives, technology is deeply ingrained into their DNA. There has always been a cheaper, faster, more entertaining way of doing things coming around the corner at them and thus they have become adaptable in a way that previous millennials may not be. Having encountered so many new applications, media modes and software in such a short amount of time has meant intuitively acquired skill sets amongst younger millennials that older generations might have received lengthy training for. They are all designers, storytellers, photographers, marketers, event organizers, sound mixers, and PR aficionados simply because they have Snapchat, WordPress, and the like. Employers can leverage this second-nature tech familiarity to affect change within an organization by encouraging conversations about new technologies and their possible uses.

Studies have determined that the older millennials tend to have less concern about underperformance or being evaluated for their work output. Because they began their career during a time of prosperity, when the focus was squarely on following your career dreams, the intrinsic motivation to pursue and find fulfilment at work is considered tantamount to any system of assessment or evaluation. The younger millennials began university or college when competition was at an all-time high and know that a perfect job may require an advanced degree or climbing a few more rungs of the ladder.

Younger millennials tend to see having a breadth of experience in their career as more beneficial than having narrow and deep expertise. Older millennials were raised by parents who, on average, stayed at jobs for long periods of time and they consider the value of seniority as something worth aiming for, *if* they're with the right organization. The younger millennials, partially as a result of their age of course, are looking to build a diverse skill set in the hopes that they may eventually

Both ends of the millennial spectrum value experiences and connection; the traditional symbols of success are becoming more and more identified as characteristic of senior managers and (gasp) parents.

find or create a unique position that calls on their varied strengths and utilizes their individual capabilities for full effect. They want jobs that provide them with an experience, a new network and some opportunities to stretch themselves. The older group wants this too, but are also keen to beef up their resume with longitudinal experience as a means to advancing their career.

There are also differences across the millennial generation in what they consider to be a luxury or necessity. Cell phones and other connectivity tools are considered absolute necessities by those in their twenties and they might feel less focused on high-end cars or designer wristwatches as markers of success. As the thirty-something's take on the managerial and more senior roles, the compensation conversation may include more discussion about development, growth, title, and opportunities to lead, with compensation that will help them support their young families.

Both ends of the millennial spectrum value experiences and connection; the traditional symbols of success are becoming more and more identified as characteristic of senior managers and (gasp) parents. They like feedback, yes, this has been a well-documented refrain about millennials. The older ones would feel most comfortable having it communicated to them in an explicit way, for example, "I really appreciate your hard word on that report, Lisa. You really took the data in an interesting direction and we will refer to it at our next board meeting." The younger group, on the other hand, may tend to prefer a more inclusive, casual demonstration of recognition, for example, "This team has produced some amazing results lately. Any ideas on how we can celebrate?"

In trying to avoid painting all millennials with the same brush, we realize that we have made our fair share of generalizations here. The point is that millennials entered their careers at different times, and under different circumstances, depending on which end of the generation they fall into. This has had an impact on their outlook on their work, on business, their goals for the future, and their style of relating to one another. It's worth examining the differences between these two groups in order to better engage your younger talent and build highly motivated teams.

Five Ways to Inspire Loyalty

Are you frustrated by what looks like a lack of loyalty in today's employees? Most of us are familiar with younger or millennial workers who change jobs frequently; some estimates are every eighteen months. Their impatience to get ahead and advance with promotions and more pay can keep their employers up at night. There's no denying these realities, and everyone can tell a story of the new hire who left almost as soon as they started.

The prevalence of more frequent job changes is not an experience unique to millennials, though. Shifting workplace demographics, mergers, acquisitions, downsizing, and offshoring mean that shorter job tenure is common across the board, regardless of level of position or industry. Often people have to change employers due to decisions not of their making; at the same time, when no further growth opportunities are present, it's natural to go after a more challenging role.

What does loyalty look like in this new normal? The pervasiveness of workplace change calls for a significant shift in mindset and a reframing of what loyalty means. It means building a culture and organization that makes people want to sign up for longer than they intended when they joined. It's time to acknowledge that for as long as people are with your organization, they should have the best possible experience they can.

Here are five building blocks for reframing a new age of loyalty:

1. **Focus on Transparency.** Regardless of the size of your company, you need to regularly update your team on current successes and struggles. If you're too selective (only sharing part of the story or only reciting what's already known through the gossip mill), employees will catch on and their trust in your leadership will wane. Regular company town hall meetings, leadership communications (meetings, email, etc.), and management visibility go a long way to making and keeping your people part of the story.

2. **Reward and Recognize.** Take opportunities to appreciate your staff in ways that are personally suited to them. Not everyone has the same desire for public recognition, and a gift card to the local coffee shop may mean more to some people than it does to others. Ask questions to find out how people most like to be recognized and then, when they do great work, make the effort to show them that you noticed.

3. **Clear the Path for Growth and Development.** Have regular conversations with your employees so you know what short and long-term goals they have for themselves. Be positive but realistic when you talk about future career and learning opportunities. Be an advocate for their development and take the time to advise them on ways to overcome any real or perceived barriers to their growth and advancement.

4. **Be Flexible.** Some workplace rules and policies are essential, and consistency in their application is even more important. At the same time, when faced with ad hoc or random requests from your people, it's important to assess every situation on its own merits and respond accordingly. By allowing for flexible schedules, changes to the work environment and supporting people's real-life struggles, you're demonstrating that your organization cares about the individual employee, and chances are the individual will care right back.

5. **Loosen Up.** Let fun happen. A couple of annual staff parties won't cut it when it comes to engaging employees on a social level. The reality is, sometimes just being open to the idea that some significant team building might emerge out of an impromptu lunch hour Frisbee tournament or an unexpected walking meeting can really affect the culture in the workplace. As a leader, it's important to participate in the fun once in a while, and maybe even instigate it!

These tips are the starting points and can seem simple on the surface and be quite another matter to implement consistently. Awareness of these strategies and instilling accountability for action across the leadership team can dramatically change your culture to one where people are thrilled to come to work every day, and won't even think about making a change when a friend reaches out with a new opportunity.

It's important to acknowledge the other side of loyalty: the individual's responsibility for their own engagement. Everyone is ultimately in charge of their own satisfaction at work and must take matters into their own hands to seek out feedback when they need it, ask for clarity when priorities or roles seem fuzzy, and connect with others to create their own sense of community. To that end, it's all easier to do in an environment that fosters such loyalty, where leaders have set the stage for individuals to feel safe, valued, and respected.

Re-recruit from Basic to Brilliant

An energizing, inclusive workplace drives high levels of engagement over the long term. Corporate values are increasingly important in defining work culture. Leaders and teams have a collective role to play in developing and sustaining collaborative working relationships.

Assess the Basics:

> Employees are kept informed about the organization's current and future strategy, direction, and business drivers.

> There are town-hall style communication events led by senior leaders, typically held quarterly or semi-annually.

> Regular management and team meetings provide opportunities for real-time issues to be addressed. Weekly and monthly meetings are a focal point for communication intended to create common ground and understanding of expectations and accountabilities.

> There is a culture of flexibility that includes varied hours for workday start and end times and other alternatives such as remote arrangements.

> Individual talents are acknowledged and celebrated through recognition and rewards. There is sincere appreciation for individual and team contributions.

➤ There are regular company social events for team members and leaders to get to know each other. There is often an employee-driven social committee in charge of planning and organizing.

➤ Conflict situations or difficult interpersonal issues may go unattended for periods, contributing to disengagement or employee departures. If managers are not accountable to address tough situations, morale can deteriorate, leading to increased absences and a decline in effort and productivity.

➤ In strongly sales-focused organizations, manager performance and compensation is generally based on revenue and profit results, even though the ability to develop a highly engaged team is essential to success.

Accelerate with Brilliance:

➤ Managers initiate periodic one-on-one conversations with their team members to take the pulse on how the individual views the work experience and what might be done to make it even better.

➤ Leader performance is assessed broadly and encompasses accountability for engaging and retaining a strong team, in addition to meeting or exceeding financial results.

➤ Most employees are able to respond positively and quickly to the question, "What keeps me here?"

➤ Managers uncover opportunities for team members to do more of what they love to do. They are deliberate in creating a strong, trusting relationship with each team member.

➤ Corporate values are established and guide expectations for behaviour and results. Every team member can articulate what they are and the meaning behind them.

➤ Communication from senior leaders and management takes many forms from weekly town halls at a company lunch, to the extensive use of social media, and intranet communication.

➤ The physical environment is an enabler of workplace positivity. Appropriate space design, proper lighting, and ergonomic furnishings support sustained productivity. Snacks, beverages, and quiet areas are available to take needed breaks and stay energized.

➤ For mid-size organizations, an employee net promoter score (EPNS) may be used to assess the degree to which current staff would be willing to recommend their employer to a friend as a great place to work. An adaptation of a customer net promoter score, the EPNS is a pulse taker on workplace satisfaction and engagement.

➤ Exit interviews are conducted when employees leave the organization to determine what if any, workplace factors may have contributed to their decision. The feedback provided is carefully considered in making improvements to the work environment.

Re-recruit Innovator: Supernova Salon

"We Train You, We Grow You, We Retain You."

Supernova Salon is hair salon with a difference. Based in North Vancouver, British Columbia, its name and tag—#loveyourhair—reflect the excellence and inspiration embodied by owner and Creative Director Dana Lyseng and her team. Lyseng is an accomplished, international award winning stylist, consistently a finalist in the Canadian Hairdressing Mirror Awards and Salon Magazine's Contessa Awards, and is a platform artist with the prestigious Wella Top Stylists team for Canada.

She had a clear vision for her business model from the outset, one that's a world apart from other salon operators in the hair and cosmetic services industry. Most salon operators own or lease their space and rent their chairs to freelance stylists who pay a monthly fee for the use of the facilities. Lyseng has taken a different approach. She set out to attract, train, and build a fully aligned, empowered, and exceptionally talented team, capable of delivering world class creativity and client service. She initially launched and grew her business with six stylists in a small strata space where she operated successfully for many years.

As the business kept growing, it became evident there was a new level of business waiting to be tapped. Looking for her next challenge, Lyseng made the leap to a fully custom designed (also award-winning) space that would allow her to scale the business, transform the brand, and make an even bigger impact. In an industry where turnover is constant and loyalty rarely heard of, Supernova Salon today boasts twenty-two employees, all selected, onboarded, trained, and fully supported to reach their potential in an environment that challenges, engages, and re-recruits every day.

Supernova's culture of engagement is carefully crafted one employee at a time, from the hiring process through onboarding and ongoing skill development. New hires are given in-depth and structured training that goes far beyond essential tasks; they are integrated in a way that allows them to embrace fully the Supernova culture and philosophy. A foundation of the culture is that every person, regardless of their role, has three clients. One is the group who has their hair done, a second are those who do hair, and the third is the entity of the business—"ourselves as a team."

There are three different job roles within the salon: the front desk team, the apprentice team, and the hair dressing team. Each job role has a different onboarding process, and what links them is the effort made to integrate every new team member into the verbal culture of the salon. Lyseng has documented onboarding and culture documents to explain the business to all who are fortunate to work there. There are a series of phrases and "right words" that exemplify the culture and service philosophy. No one says "no" or "can't"; it's "my pleasure" and "will do." Every effort is made to eliminate situations where people interpret information and "spit it out" their own way. Their language of interaction must be fully adopted and practiced. As new hires come to appreciate this difference, they value the specialness of what it means to work there and see the delight with every client, and the volume of business that comes through the door every day. There's an undeniable buzz of high energy, excitement, and engagement in the staff and clients alike.

Lyseng's experience is that millennials, the age cohort represented by most of her team, and the youngest ones in particular, have a steeper learning curve to understand Supernova's service philosophy. Many have had part-time jobs at Starbucks or Chapters/Indigo or other retail establishments, which Lyseng calls "unrelationship-based businesses." She champions a gold standard that every client who walks in the door should be a person you'd want to treat to a special dinner and evening, and every person who greets or works with that client needs to get to know the person well enough to understand what would make the Supernova experience special for them.

Another cultural differentiator is the importance placed on learning and development. Once individuals have mastered their core responsibilities, their training has only just begun. The front desk team members routinely take retail classes to become more knowledgeable about hair products. The apprentices, true to their role, participate in weekly classes where a model is chosen and a topic selected, and Lyseng teaches them what they need to know. The apprentices practice these techniques to perfection over a sixteen-week period. In addition, they learn the art of a great client consultation, including how to ask the right questions

The goal is for everyone to advance through the early stages of "I want to be confident," to "I am confident," to "I want to teach it to others."

so they can deliver exactly what the client wants. For the hairdressers, every quarter, a guest representative from a manufacturer provides an education session on the latest trends in hair styling, tools, and new product development.

The hairdressers learn to impart their knowledge to the apprentices by grasping teachable moments. It's the living example of team members valuing each other in the same way as a paying client, and need to be valued as such. The goal is for everyone to advance through the early stages of "I want to be confident," to "I am confident," to "I want to teach it to others."

The hairdressers have a ladder of development they can customize to fit their interests. From recent graduate, to intermediate, senior, and master stylist levels, the learning journey is continuous and Supernova's cultural identity helps them advance to the next level if they are motivated to do so. Lyseng's view is that hair dressing is like yoga—you practice to be good; and you get better the more you do it. As the hairdressers approach the Master level, they are encouraged to enter competitions nationally and internationally to hone and measure their expertise on the world stage.

Lyseng embodies this philosophy. She's an advisor for Wella Professionals one week per year, competes in five international competitions annually, and typically puts in eight or more hours per day at the salon.

It's the people issues that require ongoing mastery. Lyseng has established a routine of Friday morning team meetings every other week. On the Fridays in between, she rotates a schedule of one-on-one meetings with each team member. The intent is to create a place of accountability for herself, a forum of discovery where she gets to know what people need to stay engaged in the work and their own development. These meetings are a way to pre-empt anything that can come up, especially if there are budding interpersonal or teamwork issues. With a total time investment of two business days per month, they have been a game changer for her and the business and contribute significantly to building strong morale.

Lyseng has also retained the services of a business coach and with that support has "learned to talk in a curious language, and how to read my people. I need to show up as a leader in every way and continually show them this is the platform for what we do, here's how it works." Her approach has been the point of difference to her business and leadership success, the development of the Supernova culture, and the retention of her very talented team. "As an owner, you need to know who you want to be; figure out who you want to work for you, and then the kind of clients you want and the experience you want to provide."

If you hire people just because they can do a job, they'll work for your money. But if you hire people who believe what you believe, they'll work for you with blood, and sweat, and tears.

- Simon Sinek, *Start with Why*

8 Total Rewards

How can your small business go from basic to brilliant when it comes to rewarding and recognizing your people? Even with market competitive compensation and benefits, with business growth, ongoing hiring, and the evolving diversity of your people, it's a challenge to reward and recognize in a way that satisfies everyone. Take a fresh look at how your rewards are keeping pace by considering these three benchmarks.

Reflect on your corporate values and what you're trying to achieve as an employer. This is essential to selecting rewards that align with what's most important. For example, in a hard-driving sales-focused organization, rewarding outstanding sales performance with higher dollar incentives may be appropriate. If employee health and wellness is championed as an important driver of performance, then you may want more of your rewards to provide ways for individuals to enhance their self-care and personal wellness. If technology is core to your business and staying ahead of innovation and product development are mission critical, then offering additional training and the latest technology tools may be a primary rewards focus. If being a good corporate citizen underpins your corporate brand, then offering opportunities for employees to volunteer for charitable causes or community events will be highly valued. Whatever your goals as an employer, your rewards can be a way to show employees that what you offer is an expression of what you believe.

Take a close look at your employee demographics. Chances are there's diversity here, from recent college or university graduates to young millennials, mid-career professionals, and more tenured individuals not far off from retirement. Their personal situations will definitely affect the kinds of rewards that are meaningful. Some will have young families and are looking for flexibility in how and where they work; others are singularly career focused and want to develop professionally and earn the corresponding monetary rewards. Dual-career couples with families may not have time to get everything done and value connections to services and individuals who can help them take care of their daily personal activities (such as laundry, housekeeping, grocery shopping, house repairs). Is a retirement savings plan with matching employer contributions something that will be valued by all your people? If you're not sure what's important to them, just ask. The more aware you are of what they need and want, the more you'll be able to select and target total rewards that excite and keep them engaged.

Consider your budget and the financial resources available to invest in rewards and recognition. Can you afford a lavish and creative compensation program that awards trips, an all-expense paid weekend away, or cars to employees in recognition of an anniversary or significant achievement? Would it be more feasible to give a restaurant gift certificate, occasional spa days, a birthday day off, house cleanings, and repair services, or catered lunch on Fridays? Remember that supporting a workplace that rewards employee loyalty and above and beyond performance can be a significantly lower investment than the costs of staff turnover or the inability to attract and hire great people. Even if you need to stick to low cost or no-cost rewards, there are many options to consider in building your program.

In a full employment marketplace, your total rewards offering is an important lever in attracting, hiring, and retaining the best people. For the small to mid-market enterprise or non-profit organization, it can be challenging to go beyond competitive pay and bonuses, flex time scheduling, and a core offering of employee benefits. Taking a broader and more creative look at what's possible with total rewards can distinguish your organization as a best in class employer in your industry. Regardless of the rewards you choose, their success depends on full communication and implementation strategies to ensure everyone is aware of what's available to them and why.

Total rewards do more than keep your best people; they energize your workplace, instill a sense of pride, and nurture employee engagement that directly translates to the customer experience. Your employees, prospective new hires, and ultimately your customers will recognize that the leaders of your organization truly care for their people. It shows when individuals are surrounded by an employee experience that makes their lives easier, healthier, more enjoyable, and above all, more productive.

Some Facts about Total Rewards:

> For small to mid-market companies, the average annual cost of providing extended health and insurance benefits is $4,000 to $4,500 per full-time employee. These costs don't include vacation time or other rewards. Balancing cost containment to offer competitive benefits plans is a significant challenge for employers (Conference Board of Canada).

> Health-care spending accounts are becoming more common as some employers replace benefits and insurance plans to provide maximum flexibility to their staff, or they offer this benefit as a top up to 80% of benefits premium coverage. This allows individuals to personalize how they allocate their health-care spending.

> To respond to increasing cost inflation of benefit premiums, employers and employees co-share the costs. Through education and communication, employee engagement increases with a more complete understanding of how the program works and the financial investment required.

> Initial data from the ongoing Wellness Return on Investment study being performed by Sun Life and the Ivey Business School shows that employee wellness programs save about 1.5 to 1.7 days in absenteeism per worker over twelve months, or an estimated $251 per employee per year.

> A recent study by Price Waterhouse Coopers estimates that 50% of employees are distracted by their personal finances at work and spend on average three hours per work week dealing with their finances. Only 15–20% of Canadian employees have access to employer supported or group registered retirement savings plans (RRSPS).

> Educational benefits matter to younger employees and can be a definite incentive for more experienced staff to keep their skills sharp. Tuition reimbursements within a set annual budget and professional accreditation fees are common.

> Quality of Workplace rewards can vary from a travelling snack cart with healthy options, catered lunches, summer barbecues, pets allowed in the workplace, 50/50 fundraising draws that offer a cash payout, or draw prizes for weekend getaways or various gift cards.

Non-Traditional Benefits and Perks: Indulgent or Essential?

Some employers today are complementing their traditional benefits programs with unique perks and employee incentives that reflect their company's core values and commitment to a positive work environment. While the old guard may find this new trend impractical and indulgent, study after study has shown that staff engagement and retention can be significantly impacted by non-traditional benefits and perks. The good news is there are creative approaches that can be implemented simply and affordably to meet the rapidly changing expectations of employees and improve the culture of your workplace.

Why Now?

Millennials are now the largest age cohort in Canada's workforce and more than 15% have advanced to supervisory or leadership positions. Those numbers are going to grow significantly over the next five to ten years so there is little doubt that these are the people to please to maintain a progressive and vital workforce. These current and future employees of your company (and every company) are quite different to their predecessors when it comes to their work style. They have been brought up on collaboration and instant gratification. Their desire to emotionally and socially connect to their work (and their workplace) is stronger than it has ever been with past generations. They seek out opportunities to contribute and be recognized. A workplace that reflects their inclination toward camaraderie and multi-tasking will likely see a pay-off in the innovation and productivity departments.

Work/Life Balance

The nine to five world of work that so many of us are used to is a thing of the past. Prospective employees are now asking hiring managers point blank, "If I accept this position, will I need to be in the office every day?" The resulting answer could have a significant impact on their level of interest in the position. The way people view the concept of a career is changing, and along with that goes a shift in how professionals want to be compensated and rewarded. By offering perks and benefits that can support a better balance, a company is saying, "We recognize your need and want to help you achieve it." Some examples of non-traditional benefits that organizations might provide include a smartphone stipend, travel discounts or hotel vouchers, telecommuting options, casual dress code, reduced summer hours, birthdays off with pay, paid time off for volunteer commitments or community involvement, and perhaps, most significantly, flexible schedule options. Recent studies have shown that flexible work environments are so important that close to 50% of those currently working would be willing to give up a percentage of their salary for it. Too many employers talk the talk about work/life balance but do not walk the talk. The inclusion of these kinds of non-traditional benefits into an employment agreement will demonstrate an employer's commitment to what can sometimes be an empty promise.

Health and Wellness Re-defined

While extended health benefits are certainly expected and appreciated by most employees, there are additional bonuses that align nicely with a twenty-first century focus on mental, physical, and spiritual well-being. Consider providing time and space for workers to really get away from it all, if only for an afternoon. The result may be a re-energized team with higher morale and more innovative ideas.

Food is always a welcome perk, but why not encourage some gastronomic exploration instead of the same old bagel tray? An office might consider serving a healthy breakfast buffet for employees, bringing in a blender and fresh produce for smoothie Tuesdays, or organizing soup and salad delivery once a month. The offer of a couple of nourishing, ready-made family take-home meals can mean a great deal to the busy parents on your team. Health club memberships and spa certificates could be a great health incentive and possibly ease the aches and pains that your staff might incur during their daily routine.

Recognition and Growth Rewards

Many organizations are willing to cover some or all of the cost of continuing education courses if the subject matter relates to the employee's position or industry. A new trend sees companies funding their employee's further learning and development regardless of the subject matter. The expectation is that, when workers are fueling their own passion projects and personal interests, they will be more fulfilled. The act of learning, in itself, can inspire and motivate people in diverse ways.

Business leaders realize that providing training and learning activities to employees demonstrates an interest in the future growth of the individuals and the team. One-on-one meetings with individual employees where the focus is on performance success, recognition where it's due, professional growth potential, and career mapping activities, help reinforce the company's commitment to an individual's learning path.

The next generation of workers are used to regular feedback and tend to appreciate being praised and rewarded in visible ways. With some creativity, companies can find fun ways to say "job well-done." Use of a company car for a month, a premier parking spot, tickets to a sporting or social event, lunch made or delivered by the president: these are all inexpensive, yet high-impact rewards and perks that will be remembered by recipients and their colleagues for a long time to come.

Benefits to Ease the Busy-ness of Life

Anyone who works a busy Monday to Friday schedule can tell you that some of life's more mundane tasks are difficult to get done. Picking up dry cleaning, personal postage and shipping errands, carwashes, haircuts, grocery shopping, and pet-care are some of the routines employers could support in some way. Allowing employees to leave an hour early (periodically) to run errands or organizing a pick-up/drop-off service of some sort could go a long way to easing the burden of these seemingly menial though essential tasks. It may also reduce distraction and absenteeism from workers who could be finding other ways to fit these tasks into their workday.

A key consideration when implementing a non-traditional benefits or perks program should be fairness. If you can't customize benefits for individuals, be sure to choose the ones that can be utilized by everyone in some way.

While some may continue to think of non-traditional employee benefits as nothing more than an additional expense, savvy leaders know that the long-term advantages can greatly outweigh those up-front costs and contribute to your overall success. The conventional offerings such as health insurance, vacation plans, and fair to above-average compensation will always be popular, but providing an environment where employees feel appreciated, engaged, and maybe even a little bit pampered will help you retain talent and attract stronger candidates as your business grows.

Total Rewards: The Real Employment Deal

Bruce, a senior manager in a mid-sized engineering firm, has been actively involved in the hiring process for a project engineer. After many interviews, he's extended an offer to a promising candidate, Josh. The offer includes a base salary of $90,000, plus a range of employee benefits. After a brief deliberation period, Josh has just called Bruce to let him know that a competitive firm has offered him $95,000, and he's decided to accept that offer.

While Bruce had resigned himself to the fact that someone out there will always be able to offer more, he couldn't help but wonder what else he could have done to close the deal. After all, it appears there was only a difference of $5,000 annually, and he would have been willing to negotiate on that point. Were there other ways to illustrate the benefits of working with his company that might have won the candidate over? He pondered whether their compensation offerings were really out-of-sync, but ultimately concluded that they were within market rates.

What's going on in the offer process when you've done all your homework and truly believe that what you're offering is a fair and equitable salary, but somehow it's still not enough? The back story, the one that wins the day with your most talented prospective hires, is all about total rewards.

To get out of the race to the top on salaries, organizations need to become more aware of the ways they can use a total rewards concept effectively—not only for their existing employees, but also for their potential employees.

By selling your total rewards package effectively, you will show candidates the true employment deal, not just the number on their pay cheque. Candidates will have a much fuller understanding of what they will receive if they join your organization. It also takes away some pressure during the salary negotiation process as now the emphasis is on the overall value of the offer.

Here are some tips to ensure you're maximizing your organization's total rewards programs to attract and land the best candidates.

Start by detailing of all elements of your rewards offer. Chances are your rewards package will include some if not all of the following:

- **Compensation:** Annual base salary is often the focus of most offers. However, many organizations also offer short-term and/or long-term income incentives. Sometimes it can be difficult to demonstrate the value of an incentive plan, especially when it's an equity-based plan (stock options, for example). However, it can be advantageous to explain to candidates what the payout could be in different scenarios. Also, don't forget some of the extra incentives your organization may provide, such as a profit sharing, team performance bonuses, project completion bonuses, or recognition awards.

- **Benefits:** Extended health benefits are usually summarized for easy reading by the benefits provider or broker. For those organizations with a retirement savings benefit, the biggest opportunity is to make it easy for candidates to understand its value. Don't just present the plan text, include a few scenarios and real examples so new recruits can appreciate its significant potential value to them. Even for a straightforward group RRSP, instead of simply indicating that your organization contributes three per cent of base salary, why not show it in real dollars based on earnings and help them understand the potential future value? Powerful stuff.

- **Work–life Integration and Community Contribution:** Work-life programs can range from flextime and telecommuting to health and wellness initiatives to community involvement and volunteering programs. These programs usually reflect the organization's culture and values, which for many candidates can be the real differentiator for choosing their next employer.

- **Performance Mastery:** It may seem strange to include this as a reward, but the focus of the performance process has now shifted to one of shared accountability between manager and employee. An employee can benefit professionally from a well-designed and well-executed performance process that includes goal-setting measures to support their career development, strength assessments to identify undiscovered capabilities, and regular coaching to help them perform at their best.

- **Development and Career Opportunities:** One of the most common reasons candidates consider joining a new organization is for more professional growth and advancement. Some learning and development programs can be easily translated to a dollar value to show to candidates. Others may be more difficult, such as formal coaching programs, career development initiatives, mentor partnerships or cross training arrangements. For the right employee, these programs and opportunities are invaluable.

Once you're able to bring your rewards to life, you may want to create several descriptions that are customized based on your frequent hires and/or targeted demographic groups. For example, sales employees may be motivated by the incentives they receive and the scalability of their rewards; customer service staff may be more interested in flexible hours, learning opportunities, or a very competitive branch bonus plan. Whatever they are, make sure you present the most relevant rewards in a way that will best engage each candidate group.

Make sure you're giving your hiring process the best chance of success. Emphasize and honour the total rewards that you offer, and you'll see more enthusiasm from your prospective new hires.

Total Rewards from Basic to Brilliant

Compensation has evolved from "show me the money" to a total rewards strategy that supports a life of fulfillment, where base salary is only one factor. Rewards and recognition are customized for maximum benefit to individuals and the organization.

Assess the Basics:

- ➤ Employee benefits (in the form of extended health and dental coverage) are seen as a cost of being an employer and a social or moral obligation to provide some level of insurance to staff.

- ➤ The language used to describe benefits is couched in insurance-ese that can be difficult to understand.

- ➤ In an effort to show generosity, employers may pay 100% of benefit plan premiums. This can result in an entitlement mentality as staff take their benefits for granted.

- ➤ Benefits plan design is decided for employees (the big brother approach where the organization conveys that it knows what's best). The plan is often core or basic in design and benefits, often referred to as a transactional benefit plan.

- ➤ Benefits plan design is often performed as a purely administrative task separate and apart from other people strategies (such as recruitment and retention).

> Compensation beyond base salary, known as variable pay, often takes the form of profit sharing delivered through a fiscal or calendar year-end bonus payment. Bonus payments are calibrated according to the level of position an individual holds.

> There is little if any benchmarking of base salaries and variable pay (bonuses and incentives) with industry comparables.

Accelerate with Brilliance:

> Total rewards are designed to align corporate vision and values with the employee experience. There is a holistic view of all compensation.

> There is a push to provide a customized experience for each employee, driven by flexibility that gives individuals a choice in the benefits most valuable to them, such as gym memberships, bus passes, yoga classes, vision care, or paramedical services such as massage, chiropractic, or physiotherapy.

> Information and updates on benefits plans are easily accessible, often with 24/7 access through employee portals and mobile apps, along with regular updates and strategies communicated through structured face-to-face presentations.

› Investments in leadership development and soft skills training recognize the importance of professional growth for all individuals at every stage of career.

› Volunteerism and community activism are highly valued. On an annual basis, several hours or days are made available to volunteer or host fundraising events on an individual, team, or company basis. This can include contributing to green initiatives or supporting various non-profit causes and campaigns.

› A group RRSP matching program (where the employer matches employee retirement savings contributions as a percent of base salary) demonstrates a commitment to the long-term financial well-being of all staff. Each employee receives a confidential annual consultation with the plan advisor on their personal financial situation and how the program can help them reach their goals.

› Leaders understand that no matter what monetary rewards are in place, individuals need to feel valued and recognized for their contributions. Personal thank yous and kudos from one's manager are often viewed as the most valuable reward of all.

› Variable pay structures are reviewed annually. There is a focus on specific job functions to accommodate changes in the scale and nature of work output, and a renewed look at what constitutes high performance.

Total Rewards Innovator: RIMEX Supply

RIMEX

In the world of heavy industrial big-boy toys, RIMEX is hands down the leading innovator of the largest engineered wheel applications on the planet. They are the premier manufacturer of wheels and rims for the world's most challenging industrial applications in the forestry, mining, and construction industries. Their continual innovations have propelled wheel/rim technology into the future; their best of class patented Tyre-Sense wheel sensor technology is at the forefront of tire pressure monitoring systems (TPMS), capable of enduring the most uncompromising conditions inside heavy mining and construction sites. Reduced down time, lower maintenance costs, and greater safety are just a few of the reasons why RIMEX products are leading the way for rims and wheels throughout the industrial world.

The RIMEX organization is a group of companies that employs approximately 350 people globally, with primary operations in Canada, the US, and Australia, and a facility in China that employs up to a hundred, depending on product flow. With twenty company-owned sales and inspection/repair centres around the world guaranteeing 24/7 support, RIMEX strives for shared success with its customers, wherever they may be.

RIMEX Supply Canada, based in Surrey, British Columbia, employs 150 and is the headquarters for their main manufacturing operations, corporate services, and IP (intellectual property) management.

Since its founding in the 1970s by Chris Weston, the company has built a loyal and highly trained workforce. The stability of company ownership has been assured through planned succession. The founder's son Derek Weston assumed the reins of CEO approximately one year ago, now supported by a seven-person executive team. The company has always had minimal employee turnover; at the same time, growth has demanded they modernize their hiring practices to employ higher caliber talent. They've also developed a full hire-to-retire strategy for employing, developing, and rewarding their people.

Their total rewards philosophy is first evident in their hiring practices. Shortages of skilled trades are the bane of the manufacturing industry; to meet this challenge, RIMEX commits to full financial support for individuals hired into their apprenticeship programs. While this is a talent

> **Such a rigorous meeting structure is a daily opportunity to keep people informed, invite their input, and ensure they know where to focus.**

attraction strategy initially, it's very much a reward strategy as well, as individuals acquire specialized skill sets that set the stage for long-term career growth.

Individual and team performance with corresponding recognition strategies are core to their manufacturing operations. The company uses best-in-class industry measurement and process management tools (Lean, 6S, Kaizen), that provide daily safety, quality, inventory and production data. Every day at 8:00 AM, the lead-hands (team leaders) meet with their managers for updates on yesterday's output and a view of what today should bring. What follows is what's called a +QDIP meeting, where all 120-production staff (ten teams in all) stop for fifteen minutes and meet with their lead-hands to review yesterday's data, discuss what needs to be done today, and identify the problems they as a group are going to solve. Such a rigorous meeting structure is a daily opportunity to keep people informed, invite their input, and ensure they know where to focus. As a recognition tool, it's a way for the company to ensure every employee has a chance, daily, to speak up about what they are seeing and what can be done better.

This active engagement gives real meaning to the company's performance incentive program designed for production staff. Each person can be rewarded with up to five to eight percent of their base salary in recognition of overall manufacturing performance. These pay-for-performance incentives are based on three measures. One is the 6S score. 6S is a manufacturing method for ensuring workplace housekeeping and standardized processes that create efficiencies, fewer breakdowns, and higher levels of quality. Welding is inherently dirty and dusty with significant safety implications, so vigilance in maintaining a high-quality environment is essential. The 6S score is measured monthly in every area of the company, audited by a staff committee championed by a Lean expert, one of the company's manufacturing engineers. The process is owned and managed by staff, and members of the committee change every three months, ensuring all have an opportunity to participate in this mission-critical activity. The second measure is the quantity of pounds shipped. Last year, 16 million pounds of product where shipped. This is a final measure of production output that meets their exacting quality

> "If individuals put their hand up for a management position, just to earn more, they need to put their hand back down. You have to encourage people to take the ups and downs of management, and the real responsibilities that go with that."

standards. The third measure is safety as measured by number of days without lost work time due to illness or injury.

At the leadership level, a cornerstone of their recognition strategy is the company's significant investment in formal leadership development. As James Read, Director, Manufacturing, says, "We make it a priority to

develop front-line leaders as they are the enablers of a happy workforce."
These leaders have all completed leadership training, further supported
by an in-house training course for leaders on the shop floor. The company
also fully funds training and support for their professionally designated
staff, including extensive management training and technical engineering
courses.

From a rewards perspective, the company wants to get away from
the traditional perception of management roles where being promoted
to management means you've made it. As Read says, "If individuals put
their hand up for a management position, just to earn more, they need
to put their hand back down. You have to encourage people to take the
ups and downs of management, and the real responsibilities that go with
that." Their leaders are measured on synergies: "If there's friction on a
team, it's a reflection of their leader, full stop." Interpersonal friction will
have a negative impact on production and business results, and leaders
need to have the skills to manage the realities of people working together.
Their leadership training and development programs are a recognition of
the importance of these positions and the difference leaders are expected
to make.

Managers are then tasked with being the front line for the most
important rewards. For example, when a new hire reaches their first-year
anniversary their manager provides a gift card with a personal thank you.
The gift card isn't the big deal, just a token, but it's the opportunity for the
manager to congratulate the employee personally. The real reward is in
the conversation and acknowledgement that the individual has reached
an important milestone. Further, managers hold regular feedback and
development goal setting sessions with each team member. This ensures
their interests and aspirations are aligned with their work and ongoing
learning opportunities.

People issues will always be present in some form, mostly related to
communication trouble spots. If one area or group on the manufacturing

floor is going through problems, Read will make focused time to speak to the group. He's of the belief that in the absence of information we fill it up with the negative. To counteract misunderstandings, he fills every void with facts. He talks about core things, asks the group what he can do better. Then he turns the conversation over to the group and "they fully lambast me for five minutes. It's brilliant." Often a big organizational complaint is that people don't feel leaders are listening to them, and as a result, don't feel appreciated. Communication that is transparent, real, and comes from a place of genuine concern is the ultimate recognition.

At the organizational level, rewards and recognition come in the form of company events and achievements, posted on the company's Facebook and LinkedIn pages. There are regular updates about new hires, who just finished their apprenticeship, company developments, conferences attended, and so on. Social events are plentiful; every quarter, there's a

"It all comes down to creating a team environment and respect for people."

full staff barbecue, there's turkey and catered lunches over the Christmas season, and so on. While these rewards are good to have, Read considers them "eye candy" in the overall scheme of things.

RIMEX offers a full-suite of extended health and dental benefits, and a Group RRSP matching program. To recognize the long careers of their more seasoned staff, several who will retire in the next few years, a defined contribution pension plan has recently been introduced.

While flexible work hours—start and end times—are typical of many workplaces today, such arrangements remain difficult to do in a production environment where shifts need to start at set times. However, flexibility is part of the culture at RIMEX. Accommodations are made if an employee needs to leave early every now and then to attend to family or personal matters. This practice is not abused, and everyone knows that when flexing of their work hours is needed, the company will support them. "It all comes down to creating a team environment and respect for people."

Their next rewards frontier is wellness in the workplace. With their focus on environmental standards, cleanliness, and exceptional safety management, a culture of personal wellness—and recognition for it—can support these systems. Their question is how do you encourage wellness without being intrusive in people's lives? Not everyone wants to engage in regular exercise or fitness pursuits, and in that regard, providing role models and conversation about the need for self-care may be as far as they can go. They do want people to eat well and look after themselves. A corporate team participates in the Vancouver Sun Run every year, and there is company sponsorship for local sports teams when employees are participating. Still, there's always more that can be done.

So many companies have just enough resources in place—physical and human—to meet their current business obligations. In that scenario, there's no bandwidth to maximize effectiveness today and scale profitably for tomorrow. This makes it very difficult to embrace a total rewards philosophy that fully engages and retains talent over the long term. At RIMEX, the commitment to setting high performance goals supported by rigorous systems and structures has created the organizational capacity to innovate and grow their global presence.

When leaders use the tools available to them and are enabled to listen to their people and strive to do better everyday, a culture of reward and recognition follows. What is Read's greatest reward? He feels recognized when he "walks on the shop floor and everyone is happy, talking, and safe. I honestly mean that. That's the ultimate reward for doing what we need to be doing." Looking ahead, the road is wide open for more exploration, innovation, and achievement as the RIMEX success story and its people roar into the future.

Brilliance is the Difference Maker

Where to From Here

What was your approach to reading this book? Did you dive into one or two chapters to find a few points of inspiration and identify real action steps? Or did you read specific chapters mostly for validation that yes, you're doing all (or most) of the right things? Perhaps you read through each of the eight touchpoints to glean an understanding of the whole picture, and will now use this as your definitive guide to transforming your people practices. Regardless of approach, the journey from basic to brilliant begins with awareness of your mindset, where your organization is at, and where you'd like to be. The good news is that talent innovation and the transformation journey is accessible to every organization, one step or touchpoint at a time, regardless of size or industry.

Still wondering how to move forward? Like many worthwhile endeavours, starting somewhere—with one task, a meeting, or initial goal—can lead to the bigger gains you seek. Here are the stepping stones that can lead you and your people to a brighter place of more enjoyment, greater productivity, and larger impact:

- Start with one of the touchpoints where the greatest gains are needed or where the quickest wins can be made.
- Assess how well the basics are covered. Then, identify two or three points of brilliance that will accelerate a quick-start, building momentum for the rest. Your commitment to seeing the changes through will be key to success.
- Work with champions who share your vision for transformation. You go further by going together, and a shared vision for the future enables everyone to enjoy the view.
- Ownership and accountability will translate into true results and openness to refining as you go. Be sure to measure activities and outcomes, and course correct when needed.
- Embrace new surprises that will come from accelerating with brilliance. Agile workplaces are the most interesting and present opportunities to make the most of what's around the next corner.

Understanding and navigating the impact of your people practices is one of the most challenging aspects of leading a business. As our world becomes more complex and the structure of work continues to evolve, leaders must focus more than ever on the human talents they employ. In all the interviews, client engagements, presentations, research, and consultations that have contributed to this work, I have found the most successful companies, in particular those profiled in this book, have fully embraced the transformation journey. As a result, they have become difference makers as employers, industry leaders, and pace setters. Their brilliance, without exception, has been enabled by the following attributes.

1. They **clearly communicate the vision** of their business, the mission, purpose, and where it's heading. There is transparency and frequency in the communication, which gives clarity of purpose to all, from the warehouse worker, to the sales representative, to the IT Manager and

VP of Product Development. All know how the vision affects the work they do and the difference they make.

2. **Corporate values** are alive and well. Not just platitudes on the office wall, they are championed as the key drivers of behaviour, decision making, and how work gets done. Potential new hires are interviewed and selected for their values fit with the company.

3. They **compete on culture**. In a world where there's always a higher bidder on salary, and perhaps more advanced competitors in technology or market share, who the company is as an employer and how they treat their people is the true competitive advantage. Especially when it comes to attracting and retaining great talent.

4. They **invest in people**, heavily. Yes, monetarily, with competitive compensation and support for ongoing training and development. Beyond that, they invest in relationship development that includes mentoring with leaders, one-on-one time with executives or the owner(s), and peer learning groups. Time and energy is invested in getting to know one another, understanding key motivators, and what each person needs to give and gain value from the ongoing relationship.

5. They pay attention to the **physical work environment**. From ensuring a clean and dust-free production floor, to ergonomically designed and furnished workstations and natural light whenever possible, they know that productivity is optimized when people are comfortable in their workspace, whatever form that may take. In environments where safety is paramount, safety culture is promoted, measured, and celebrated.

6. There is a **commitment to accountability** above all. They are performance driven organizations. Everyone knows what's expected of them and how that will be measured. They measure what's meaningful, and don't fret about the rest. Accountability drives performance, performance drives results.

No organization today can afford to squander the talents of the people who place their trust in those they work for and those they lead. Your people practices should not be mysterious. They need to be intentional, purposeful, and relevant. Your efforts on this journey will shine brilliance on how you design and lead an organization that serves the business well, attracts and hires the right people, and inspires and supports them to perform at their best. This is the real sustainable, competitive advantage. May the path from basic to brilliant be your difference maker!

Acknowledgments

It really is true when authors declare that it takes the contributions of many people for a book to come to fruition! I experienced that reality very quickly as I reached out to colleagues, clients, and business advisors for their expertise and insights. Their perspectives and support have been invaluable on the publishing journey.

A tremendous thank-you to Julie Block, who elegantly played the role of designer, internal editor, reality checker, and raving book fan, in the most gracious way possible. She was instrumental in developing the Talent Innovation Diagnostic, our first online tool that lay the foundation for the eight touchpoints and the book to follow. As the project developed, she's been indispensable in staying the course as we moved from concept to publication. Aside from the sheer talent she brought to this effort, she's shown endless patience when I had none.

A special call-out to Kelly Aslanowicz who launched the first CEN-TREPOINT blog, a seminal development that built the basis for this book's content. She strongly encouraged me to capture the many insights gathered from consulting engagements and daily client interactions to share with the world at large. Her creativity and drive to think bigger about the importance of this work is a gift for which I'll always be grateful.

I am so fortunate to have partnered for many years with Diane Thielfoldt of The Learning Café, whose enthusiasm, friendship, professionalism, and deep knowledge of multi-generational workplaces and people strategies are unfailingly at the leading edge. Her insightful and thoughtful guidance and constant willlingness to share her wisdom has touched this project in more ways than she could know.

The support of an informal board of directors has brought another dimension to this work and this project, especially as a testing ground for concepts and level of commitment. Thank you to the members of my executive forum group: Jim Mathison, Rod Fram, Vince Olfert, Monika Hildebrand, Eddie Wood, Doug Vanderspek, Wes Drewlo, and Kurtis Osborne for their positive encouragement, frank talk, and good humour from my initial presentation of the concept to naming the book and navigating the writing process.

Thank you to my professional colleagues who are always ready to support and lend a hand with referrals and introductions to subject matter experts. Thank you Chris Forman, Tammy Vigue, and the Porchlight Financial team, Derek Barichievy of the Canadian Manufacturers and Exporters Association, and Kathy Enros of ACL.

I have amazing consulting clients. Every day I feel humbled by their commitment to building the strongest and healthiest organizations they can. I am grateful to each of them for sharing their journeys, their candor and vulnerability, and giving me the opportunity to help them move their businesses and people forward.

A special thank you to the leaders of the eight organizations who gave me the opportunity to profile their brilliance. You have helped shape the vision for this book and helped me say true to the reasons why organizations must never settle for basic, but embrace the path to brilliance and reap the rewards.

CREW Marketing Partners
Braden Douglas, Nick Bideshi, and James Tweedy

Ideon Packaging
Chris McDonald, Mike Nunn, Jaclyn Fisher

Mount Seymour Resorts
Eddie Wood

Clio
Rian Gauvreau and Lyndsey Hannigan

Vivo
Erin Berube and Renée Safrata

TimberWest Forest Products
Jan Marston and Jeff Zweig

Supernova Salon
Dana Lyseng

Rimex
James Read

My deepest thanks go to my husband Ernie, whose boundless support is the foundation of my life, inspiring me to bring my best everyday. He has been the biggest believer of all since day one with his never-faltering encouragement, humour, great insights, patience, and love.

About the Author

Doris Bentley understands the evolution of small to mid-market businesses and the people challenges inherent in any growing venture. For over twenty years, through the founding and growth of her own business, she has consulted and advised leaders of owner-managed businesses, non-profit and government organizations, as well as budding entrepreneurs in the chaos of business start-up.

Doris is passionate about helping leaders develop and deliver on a vision for themselves and their organizations so they can achieve their personal, professional, and business goals with clarity and confidence. By defining the work people do, assessing talent needs, recruiting perfect-fit new hires, and advancing leadership growth, she supports their commitment to see people thrive and business accelerate.

She works with clients to plan and scout the road ahead, engaging them in essential conversations to resolve their people issues without second guessing the decisions they make. Whether working with founders, CEO's, emerging or tenured leaders, she provides fresh perspectives and strategies to help them navigate their journey with wisdom and integrity.

Doris is an accomplished speaker, facilitator, and frequent presenter to various CEO and executive forum groups. As a writer and educator, she has authored many articles, blog posts, white papers, and management tool kits to advance workplace innovation and contemporary people practices.

She holds Bachelor of Arts and Education degrees, has completed graduate work in organizational development, and holds the Chartered Professional in Human Resources (CPHR) designation, along with certifications in a number of psychometric assessment instruments.

For more information, visit www.centrepointcareer.com.

CPSIA information can be obtained
at www.ICGtesting.com
Printed in the USA
LVHW04*2301100518
576815LV00002B/15/P